ENERGY
POWER FOR PEOPLE

LAURENCE PRINGLE

ENERGY

POWER FOR PEOPLE

MACMILLAN PUBLISHING CO., INC.
New York
COLLIER MACMILLAN PUBLISHERS
London

The author wishes to thank Dr. Dean Abrahamson,
Professor of Public Affairs, University of Minnesota,
for reading and suggesting changes in the manuscript of this book.

Macmillan Publishing Co., Inc., 866 Third Avenue, New York, N.Y. 10022
Collier Macmillan Canada Ltd.
Printed in the United States of America
3 4 5 6 7 8 9 10

LIBRARY OF CONGRESS CATALOGING IN PUBLICATION DATA

Pringle, Laurence P Energy: power for people.
Bibliography: p. 1. Power resources—Juvenile literature.
[1. Power resources] I. Title.
TJ153.P75 333.7 74-19033 ISBN 0-02-775330-1

CONTENTS

POWER FOR PEOPLE

1
SORRY, NO GAS

The energy shortages that struck late in 1973 caught many people by surprise. Before that time there had been only brief shortages of fuels in some areas. Then, in the span of a few months, highway speed limits were lowered, gasoline supplies ran short, airline flights were cut back, and lighting and heating were reduced in homes, schools, and businesses.

People bought small cars rather than big ones. They traveled less, and in some areas had to wait in line for hours in order to get gasoline. Some businesses suffered, and thousands of workers lost their jobs.

Some people feared the worst. A professor at the University of West Virginia predicted: "The day of Sunday, July 4, 1976, the 200th birthday of the United States of America, will dawn on a nation not in celebration but one that will be desperately trying to save itself from the crush of a collapsing economy because of a shortage of energy."

Most people were more optimistic, but they were also

Cars waiting in line for gasoline.

confused and angry about the sudden shortages of energy. They wondered how we had gotten into this mess. They wondered whether oil companies had planned the situation in order to increase profits.

Some politicians assured people that the shortages would soon be over. They were wrong. So were many economists and others who had spoken about energy supplies as early as the 1960s. A White House study in 1966, for example, had concluded that "the nation's total energy resources seem adequate to satisfy expected requirements through the remainder of the century at costs near present levels."

Actually there had been many warnings of energy shortages. As early as 1952, the President's Materials Policy Commission had warned of the "extraordinarily rapid rate at which we are utilizing our materials and energy resources." The commission recommended that the federal government develop long range energy plans. This was not done. Through the years, energy matters were studied by many government agencies and by several committees in Congress, but little was accomplished. Like most citizens, government workers and political leaders seemed to believe that energy would always be cheap and plentiful.

In the early 1970s there were further warnings of coming shortages. Nevertheless, there was still no long range planning for energy needs, and little money was being spent on energy research. When Arab nations cut off the flow of petroleum to the United States in 1973, some people blamed them for the shortages that developed. Later on it seemed that the Arabs had done the United States and

About half of the earth's known reserves of petroleum lie in the Middle East. This oil pipeline is in Iran.

other industrial nations an unintended favor—for their actions helped people realize that fuel shortages had been developing for years. They made people finally face the facts about the energy supplies of the earth.

Energy is the capacity to do work. Modern industrial nations use great amounts of energy to heat and light homes, businesses, and streets; cook and refrigerate food; run automobiles, trains, ships, and airplanes; and operate hundreds of thousands of machines and appliances in homes, schools, businesses, and factories.

Drawing by Don Wright; © 1973 Washington Star Syndicate, Inc.

The United States has grown and become a rich, powerful country because it has always had cheap, plentiful supplies of energy. At first wood was the major source of energy. It supplied more than 90 percent of our nation's energy in the 1850s. By 1900 coal had become the main fuel. And by the early 1970s, three-quarters of our energy came from petroleum and natural gas.

Today, with just 6 percent of the earth's people, the United States uses a third of all the energy produced in the world. The amount of energy we use each year has increased 30 times since 1850, and it is still growing. From the mid-1960s through the early 1970s, energy use in the United States increased almost four times faster than the population did. The growing demand for energy was caused mostly by the increased use of automobiles and electricity—two especially wasteful uses of fuels.

When the energy shortages began, people began to use fuels more carefully. But even then, people in the United States could fairly be called energy "pigs." In the early 1970s, for example, 210 million Americans used more energy for air conditioning than 800 million Chinese used for *all* purposes. Other nations, where people have a life-style more like that of the United States, use much less energy than Americans do. A person in Great Britain or Germany uses only about half as much as a person in the United States; a Canadian uses about two-thirds as much.

For many years, Americans have been encouraged to use more and more energy. This has been the message in many advertisements. Also, several government agencies and commissions, including the Federal Power Commission, have tended to promote the wasteful use of energy rather than its conservation. People have become accustomed to buying cars and appliances, building homes and other structures, and making thousands of other decisions without giving much thought to the amounts of energy needed. But that time has come to an end. For a while, as energy shortages first developed, people wondered: When can we get back to the old style of life with its cheap and abundant energy? The answer, in the opinion of many energy experts, is "never."

The petroleum age is ending. Petroleum, or crude oil, can be changed to gasoline, jet fuel, heating oil, and other products. It is an especially important fuel in the United States, where it provides nearly half of all energy needs. But oil fields in the United States are beginning to run dry. They reached their peak of production in 1971; since then the amount of oil pumped from them has dropped. But the demand for petroleum products keeps rising. So the United States depends, more and more, on other countries for its petroleum needs. This seemed to make sense when foreign supplies were cheap. But prices rose rapidly, and the Arab oil embargo showed that foreign imports cannot always be relied on.

The earth's supplies of petroleum are limited and are rapidly being used up. Even though there are huge oil fields that have not yet been tapped, the world's petroleum will be nearly gone within 50 years, according to most estimates. Even the Alaskan oil fields, the largest discovered so far in the United States, will meet all of the nation's oil needs for only a few years.

Clearly it is long past time to look for other sources of energy. The United States doesn't have far to look: it has rich deposits of oil shale, from which oil can be extracted; it also has great amounts of coal—perhaps half of the earth's known supplies. But these fuels present problems which must be solved before they can replace the dwindling supplies of petroleum and natural gas. These fuels

The Alaskan field at Prudhoe Bay contains about ten billion barrels, and more oil may be found on other parts of Alaska's North Slope. But the United States uses more than five billion barrels a year.

Wherever energy is used, the land, air, and water are often badly polluted.

cannot become substitutes for petroleum until billions of dollars are spent on research.

In the early 1950s nuclear energy was promoted as "the energy of the future." Many people believed that nuclear energy would produce almost limitless amounts of cheap power. But it has developed much more slowly than predicted. In 1973 nuclear power plants produced only about 5 percent of the electricity and less than 2 percent of the total energy used in the United States. The development of nuclear energy has been opposed at times by people concerned about public health and the quality of the environment. Environmentalists have also tried to avoid or reduce damage from other energy sources. Wastes from the production and use of energy—such as waste rock and acid water at coal mines, spilled oil from tankers and offshore wells, waste heat from power plants, and waste gases from factory furnaces, power plants, and automobiles—can do great harm to the environment.

Beginning in the 1960s, environmentalists were among those who first warned of energy shortages. They stressed the idea that the earth has limited resources, and that the wasteful lifestyle of the United States cannot go on much longer. Environmentalists supported laws aimed at cleaning up and preventing water pollution and reducing air pollution. The National Environmental Policy Act became law in 1970. It required builders of dams, power plants, highways, airports, and other projects supported by federal funds to consider the possible effects of their work on the environment.

When energy shortages developed, some people blamed environmentalists for blocking or slowing construction of power plants and oil refineries. As the facts were revealed, however, other factors, especially poor planning by utilities, energy companies, and the federal government, were found to be much more important. In 1973, the Atomic Energy Commission studied the progress of 35 nuclear plants that were being considered for operating licenses. The study showed that only one or possibly two units had been delayed for environmental reasons. All 35 had been delayed because of problems in meeting safety standards, however. A 1973 report by the Federal Power Commission

No one knows how the Alaskan oil pipeline will affect the half

reached a similar conclusion about non-nuclear power plants.

A pipeline from Alaskan oil fields was delayed by the efforts of environmentalists. Some oil company officials later admitted that the pipeline is safer as a result of suggestions from people concerned about the environment. A study by the United States Geological Survey was more blunt: it stated that the Trans-Alaskan Pipeline would have failed disastrously had it been built as originally planned by the oil industry.

Many industries are unaccustomed to considering the environmental effects of their operations. Laws such as the

million caribou that migrate through northern Alaska each year.

National Environmental Policy Act may cost them time and money. Some industry officials saw the energy shortages as an opportunity to weaken these laws. Industrial advertisements called the energy shortages a "crisis" and argued that antipollution efforts should be postponed.

But was there really a crisis? The words energy "crunch," "pinch," "squeeze," or "shortage" seemed more accurate. In fact, increasing numbers of people believe that the real problem began during the period from 1940 to 1970. People used more energy in those 30 years than they consumed in all American history before then. It was during those years that people in the United States came to believe and act as though energy would always be cheap and limitless. *That* was the crisis. The energy shortages simply forced people to face reality: we live in a world of limited resources.

Early in 1974, a government energy official spoke of his concern that the American people will go to sleep again. "They cannot continue to live their wastrel ways," he said. "Americans waste 30 to 40 percent of their energy resources and [they will] have to go through a permanent change in lifestyle."

Just what form the changes would take was unclear at first. But the changes promised to be far-reaching and to affect great energy wasters, like automobiles, the most. "The joy ride is over," said Stewart Udall, former Secretary of the Interior. "The United States automobile culture is in climax; we'll never see anything like it in the world again."

Energy shortages affect poor nations as well as rich ones. Although India, for example, uses comparatively little energy, the fuel it buys is vital for producing food and developing industry. Rises in energy costs during 1973 doubled the price of fertilizer bought by India. Yet India had been using more and more fertilizer in an attempt to grow enough grain to feed its 580 million people. If India cannot afford to import the usual amount of fertilizer, its grain harvest will be reduced. So energy shortages can cause food shortages.

The energy shortages of 1973–74 and their effects were only a preview of the challenges facing humankind. A world that depends on cheap petroleum products will have to find other sources of energy. And people who have become used to wasting energy will have to learn to use much less.

LUFKIN

PETROLEUM AND NATURAL GAS

Fossil fuels provide nearly 95 percent of the energy used in the United States and other industrial nations. These fuels—petroleum, coal, and natural gas—heat most of our homes and run our cars, airplanes, factories, mills, and railroads. In power plants they are burned to heat water, producing steam to turn turbines that generate electricity. Fossil fuels gave us the automobile age and the space age.

Most of these fuels were formed more than 300 million years ago. Coal had its beginnings in areas where plants grew in shallow marshes and swamps. Year after year dead plants fell into the water and began to decay. Layers of partly decayed matter called peat built up. Sometimes these layers were many feet thick. Eventually, as the sea rose or the land sank, deeper water covered the peat. Clays, sands, or other sediments settled out of the water and pressed down on the peat. The sediments gradually changed to sedimentary rocks, and the weight of these rocks helped to change the peat to coal.

Petroleum, like coal, is found in sedimentary rocks, but

the process of petroleum formation is not understood as well as that of coal. Most scientists believe that petroleum formed from single-celled ocean organisms called plankton, which settled to the bottom of shallow seas. Like the plants that formed coal, the plankton were only partially decayed, and they were changed by the weight of sediments. Natural gas is found with both coal and petroleum deposits; it is mostly a gas given off as once-living things decay. Coal, petroleum, and natural gas are called fossil fuels because you can sometimes find fossils (the imprints of ancient plants and animals) in coal and rocks surrounding natural gas and petroleum.

Fossil fuels are still forming through the same processes as in the past. But these fuels form so slowly that, for all practical purposes, they are nonrenewable resources. Once they are gone, substitutes must be found. Unfortunately, the fossil fuels we depend on most, petroleum and natural gas, are the ones in shortest supply.

PETROLEUM

Petroleum supplies half of the United States' energy, mostly in the form of gasoline, heating oil, and jet fuel. Many chemists believe that petroleum is too valuable to be used for heating and transportation. They would rather have petroleum reserved for use in lubricating machinery and for making petrochemicals, which are raw materials for plastics, paints, and medicines. Many people learned about the widespread use of petrochemicals when rising petroleum prices caused higher prices on thousands of

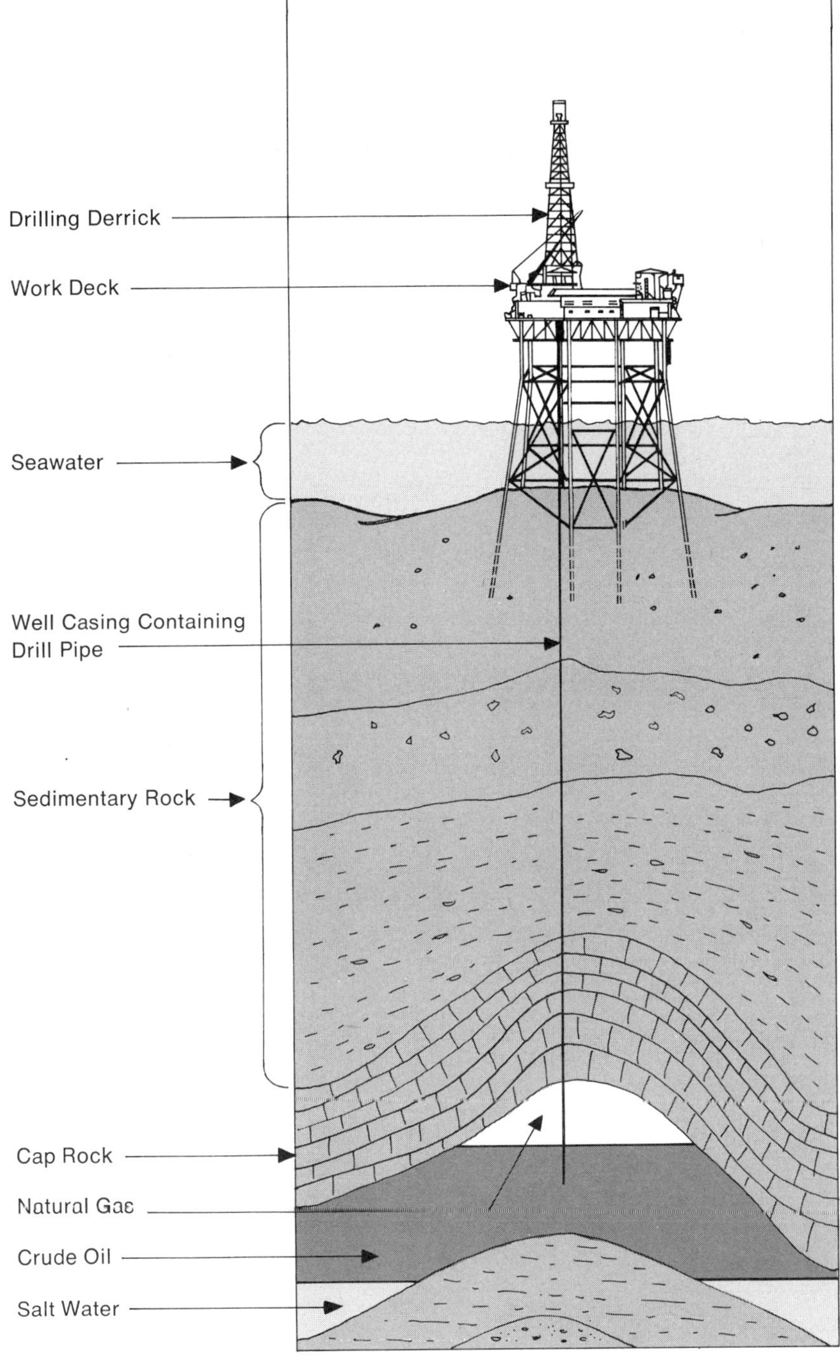

Reaching under the sea for oil and natural gas.

other products, including phonograph records, toys, vitamins, detergents, fertilizers, inks, and photographic film.

In 1973 the United States used about 17 million barrels of petroleum, or crude oil, a day. (There are 42 gallons in a barrel.) If the use of oil continues to grow as it did in the early 1970s, about 24 million barrels a day will be needed by 1980.

There is still a great deal of petroleum left in the world. There may be as much as 1,000 billion barrels, enough to last for 50 years. But most of the easily recovered oil in the United States has already been found and is being produced. The rest will come from expensive deep drilling, from remote areas in Alaska, and from wells drilled off the nation's coasts. Petroleum prices will rise as more and more of this hard-to-get oil is used.

The first offshore drilling out of sight of land took place about 1948, in the Gulf of Mexico. Now almost a fifth of total world oil production comes from offshore wells. Of the United States' remaining petroleum supplies, 40 percent is estimated to be under the outer continental shelf. The most promising Atlantic coast areas are at least 40 miles offshore and 600 feet under water.

Besides the technical difficulty of drilling for offshore oil, many people are worried about possible damage to the environment. Oil spills foul beaches and kill sea life. Areas

Some offshore wells rest on floating platforms; others stand on legs imbedded in the sea floor.

along the coast are especially rich with plant and animal life, with most ocean fish, lobsters, and other seafoods concentrated there. Offshore supplies of oil and natural gas undoubtedly will be tapped, but environmentalists are trying to prevent harmful oil spills. At a public hearing on offshore drilling, an expert on ocean fishes said, "The North Atlantic and Gulf of Alaska Continental Shelves, as well as the Gulf of Mexico, are among the world's most productive marine areas; therefore, no efforts should be spared in taking precautions to protect our Continental Shelves from oil contamination."

With the demand for petroleum still growing and the cost of imported oil rising, the federal government moved to develop more of its own supplies of oil. The United States turned to oil from Alaska, from offshore wells, and from an untouched source of petroleum—oil shale.

In 1968 the federal government had tried to auction off some oil shale lands to petroleum companies. The bids were so low that the government decided not to accept any. Early in 1974 the government tried again, and two oil companies jointly bid over $41,000 an acre, the most money ever offered for a federal mineral lease. (Even at that price, some oil experts considered the lease a giveaway.)

The huge difference in the bids of 1968 and 1974 was mostly a result of rising oil prices. In 1968 crude oil was selling for about $3 a barrel, and the cost of producing a barrel of oil from oil shale was estimated at more than $8. By 1974, however, crude oil often sold for $10 or $11 a barrel. Better ways had been found for recovering oil from

A chunk of oil shale—an abundant rock in parts of Utah, Colorado, and Wyoming. Great amounts of energy and water are needed to mine it, get oil from it, and restore the land after mining.

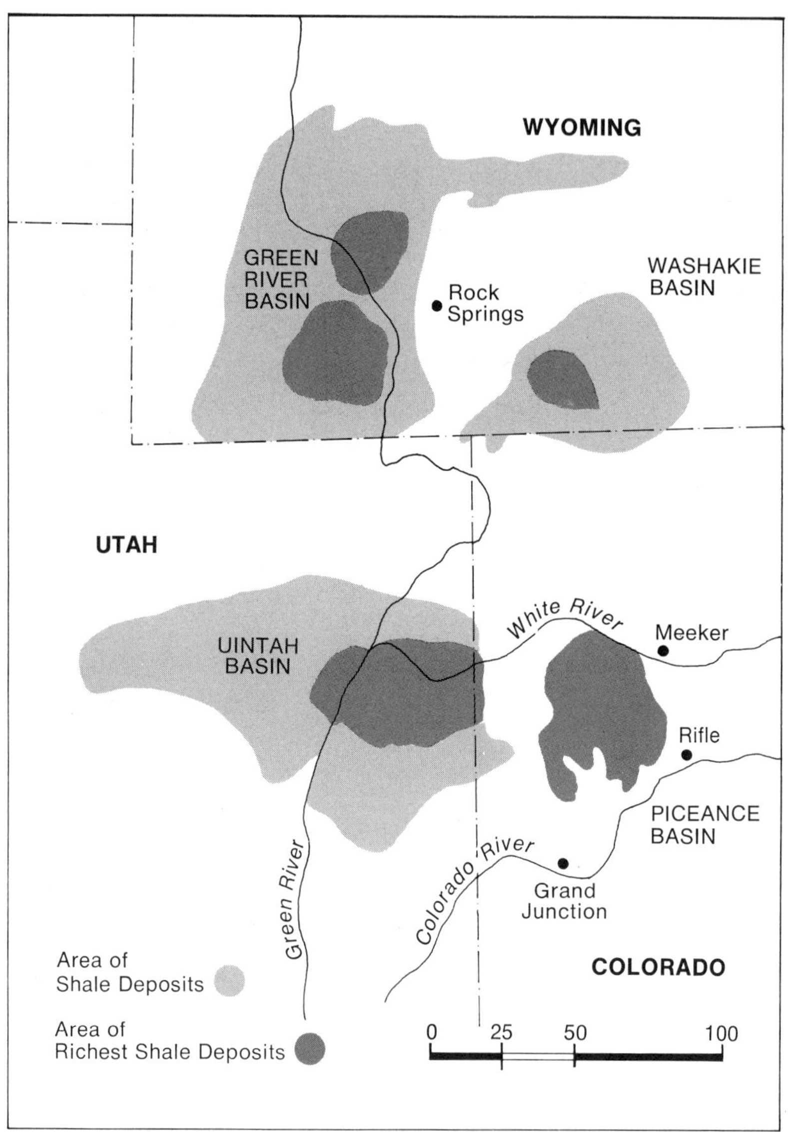

Oil shale land in the western United States.

shale, so the estimated cost of producing shale oil had dropped to $6 or less a barrel. Oil shale development had quickly become a profitable idea. The federal government leased six sites for testing of different methods of mining and processing oil shale. Some oil companies are also building oil shale plants on private land.

Oil shale is not really shale, nor does it contain oil. It is marlstone rock, and contains a tarlike material called kerogen. When the rock is crushed and heated to about 900°F (482°C), kerogen releases vapors that can be converted to oil. This oil contains great amounts of nitrogen and sulfur. Once these substances are removed (and made into useful byproducts of ammonia and hydrogen sulfide), the oil can be refined into gasoline or other petroleum products. The amount of oil that can be extracted from marlstone varies from place to place. The richest oil shales in the world yield more than 100 gallons of oil from a ton of rock. That is unusual; some shales yield only 15 gallons per ton.

Most of thc known oil shale lands in the United States are owned by the federal government, in Colorado, Utah, and Wyoming. At least 600 billion barrels of oil lie there. And now that oil shale development seems profitable, exploration will increase and more reserves may be found.

Extracting oil from marlstone is not a new idea. This kind of oil was uscd in lamps at about the time of the American Revolution. Long before then, Ute Indians in Colorado used "the rock that burns" for campfires. Oil shale has been used commercially in China, Spain, Scotland, and Estonia (USSR) for many years.

The potential value of oil shale is great, but its development also has potential for tremendous damage to the environment. Travelers in Estonia, where oil shale mining has gone on for decades, report that the landscape looks like the surface of the moon. Mountains of waste rock stand beside huge pits and scars left from strip mining.

In the United States, beds of oil shale sometimes lie just under the surface of the land. Other deposits may be 1,500 feet or more underground. If strip mining is used to get at the shale, all of the overburden—the rock and soil above the shale—must be removed and piled somewhere. According to the Department of the Interior, over seven million tons of overburden will have to be removed from one of the leased oil shale sites in Colorado. The mine pit will eventually be 1,400 feet deep. And the open pit mine will operate for 16 years before any waste shale or overburden can be put back.

Waste marlstone presents special disposal problems. It expands like popcorn as it releases its oil, and takes up more space than it did before processing. So wastes cannot simply be dumped back into the pit from which they came; they will fill that pit and there will still be huge piles of leftovers.

The full environmental impact of this kind of oil shale mining may be revealed as the first deep pit mine in Colorado is developed. A study by the Department of the Interior predicts an increase in air pollution, and admits that little is known about restoring plant life to an area after mining. This mining method will also consume great

Piles of oil shale wastes rise behind the Lenin Schistose Refining Works in Estonia (USSR).

amounts of energy. Fuels will be needed for earth-moving and mining equipment, for "cooking" the shale, and for enriching the oil. Perhaps as much as nine units of energy will be needed to produce ten units of energy from oil shale.

At three other leased sites, marlstone will be mined underground, brought to the surface, and processed there. In Wyoming, another way of recovering oil from marlstone will be tested. It is sometimes called the *in situ*, or "in place," method, and it has been used successfully on a small scale in Colorado. First a chamber is blasted deep within an oil shale formation. Then natural gas is piped into the chamber and lit. The heat of the burning gas "cooks" the oil from the shale, and the oil is pumped to the surface after it seeps to the bottom of the chamber.

The *in situ* process may recover less oil than other methods of extracting oil from shale, but it also may be much less expensive. It also seems less likely to cause much environmental damage. The surface of the land will be mostly undisturbed. Former Secretary of the Interior Stewart Udall is hopeful that the *in situ* method can be perfected. He says, "The whole western slope of Colorado is one of the finest outdoor recreation playgrounds in the country. Unless you leave the shale in the ground, how can you do anything but turn the area into a wasteland?"

The White River in Utah, near one of the areas leased for oil shale development.

Udall also warns against relying on what he calls "paper," or "armchair," energy. Development of oil shale is just beginning in the United States; no great amounts of oil will be produced until 1985 or later.

Also, the development of the six sites leased in 1974 may reveal unexpected problems that will slow oil production or even make it uneconomical. A lack of water is one possible problem. Government scientists estimate that there is enough water for oil shale processing on the six leased sites. But these sites cover only 48 square miles. There are 16,500 square miles of prime oil shale lands in Colorado, Utah, and Wyoming—and not much water. Full-scale production of oil shale might require dam-building and a system for bringing large amounts of water from other areas. This would be expensive, harmful to the environment, and difficult to arrange in a region where ranchers, farmers, and other groups already claim the right to use the fresh water supplies.

Oil shale looks very promising "on paper." If it can be developed economically and with little damage to the environment, oil shale can extend the petroleum age for many more years. *How* it is developed can make a big difference. One environmentalist said, "Until 1974 nobody was very interested in oil shale. Now the oil companies are eager to get at it. But it doesn't belong to them. It is mostly on public land. It is our land, our shale, our oil. It is worth trillions of dollars, and we must learn more about oil shale and make sure our land isn't ruined and our oil isn't sold for a song."

Natural gas being burned (and wasted) at an offshore oil well.

NATURAL GAS

Natural gas is a resource that was squandered in the past, and sometimes it is still wasted. Natural gas and petroleum often occur together, and are pumped from the same underground reservoirs. Drillers used to consider it a waste product, and burn it at the oil field. Remarkably, this still goes on. According to a trade journal of the gas industry, as much as 270 million cubic feet of natural gas is burned daily as it comes out of the ground. This usually happens where there is no gas pipeline nearby.

Natural gas is the cheapest fossil fuel because it can be used almost exactly as it comes from the ground, and it is easily transported through pipelines. It is also the least polluting since it is mostly methane (a simple compound made of four parts of hydrogen for every one of carbon). It burns more completely than petroleum or coal and leaves little waste. The demand for natural gas rose sharply as air pollution laws took effect and industries looked for a cleaner fuel than coal or oil. The use of natural gas increased 73 percent between 1961 and 1971. Utilities in 21 states had waiting lists of customers they could not supply.

In 1974, at the rate natural gas was being used, there was only about a dozen years' sure supply left in the United States. And gas was being used at about twice the rate new supplies were being found. However, the American Petroleum Institute, an organization representing most of the petroleum industry, predicted that enough other reserves of natural gas would be found for a 50-year supply, if people continued to use gas at about the annual rate of the early 1970s.

Exploration for natural gas slowed for a time because its low price, set by the Federal Power Commission, apparently kept oil companies from making much of a profit. Some critics of the oil industry believe that more reserves of natural gas had been found but were not developed until prices rose. Precious time was lost during the years when gas exploration lagged. Once a source of gas is discovered, years of work are needed before it actually produces gas for people to use.

It now appears that the United States will have to import more and more gas. Much of it will probably come from the Middle East and North Africa in special tankers. The gas is cooled to a temperature of 259°F (126°C) below zero, the point at which natural gas becomes liquid. The volume of gas shrinks as it cools, so 625 cubic feet of gas can be carried and stored as one cubic foot of liquified gas.

Ships like this bring liquefied natural gas to the United States from other parts of the world.

Pipe to be used for the Alaskan oil pipeline. Another pipeline is being planned that would carry natural gas from Alaska.

One promising new source of natural gas is methane, a dangerous gas found in some underground mines. In 1968 a methane explosion killed 78 miners in West Virginia, and this tragedy led to increased research in mine safety by the United States Bureau of Mines.

For many years powerful fans have been used to keep methane from collecting where miners are working. Each day an estimated 300 million cubic feet of methane is blown out of mines by air ventilation systems. Studies by the Bureau of Mines showed that this gas can be piped out of mines and into commercial natural gas pipelines. Engineers discovered that they could drill a small shaft down into a coal bed and remove methane two years or more

before miners worked that area. This made mining safer, and revealed a vast source of methane. The Bureau of Mines estimates that the nation's reserves of natural gas will double if all of the methane in coal beds can be recovered. This is unlikely to happen, unless rising costs of natural gas encourage coal companies to begin tapping this unexpected treasure.

The Alaskan oil fields are another source of natural gas, but certainly not a cheap or an easy one. A 3,000-mile pipeline, costing $2.5 billion, must be built before gas begins to flow to the lower 48 states. If environmental problems can be solved, this gas pipeline may be finished by the early 1980s.

Natural gas from other sources will be even more difficult to recover. Geologists believe that there are huge amounts of gas more than 15,000 feet underground. So far, the cost of drilling and the low prices for natural gas have discouraged exploration for this fuel. Beneath oil shale deposits in the western United States there is an estimated 300 trillion cubic feet of gas. It is trapped between the particles that make up sandstone rock, and oozes out slowly when wells are drilled. In 1973 the Atomic Energy Commission tried to free some of this gas by setting off three nuclear explosions more than a mile underground in the Piceance Creek Basin of Colorado. The test showed that nuclear explosions can be used to break up sandstone formations, releasing some of the gas so that it can be piped to the surface. There is doubt, however, about whether any more nuclear explosions will be used to fracture the sandstone. Hundreds of explosions would be needed to develop a large gas field. Environmentalists and other people are concerned that dangerous nuclear wastes will get into underground water, into the air, and into the natural gas itself (thereby making it unusable).

Some geologists believe that the trapped gas can be freed by forcing water, under great pressure, down shafts drilled in the sandstone. This process is called hydraulic fracturing, or hydrofracturing. The method has failed in Colorado so far, but it has not been tried on the massive scale which brought results in other kinds of gas fields.

The United States is still rich in supplies of petroleum and natural gas. But the handy sources are rapidly being used up, and decades of poor planning and poor decisions have left the nation far behind in developing new supplies. Precious years of "lead time"—the time required to find new sources and begin production—have been lost. Billions of dollars are now being spent on energy research and development, but most of the lost time cannot be made up. Fortunately the United States has another fossil fuel to turn to: coal.

1879

3

COAL COMES BACK

Coal was once king of the fuels in the United States and other industrial nations. During World War II it supplied 70 percent of our energy—used directly, as fuel for heating homes and factory furnaces, or indirectly, by power plants to produce electricity. Now it provides only about 18 percent. But with other fossil fuels getting scarce and one and one-half trillion tons of coal under American soil, it seems inevitable that coal will be king once again.

Coal will be a very unpopular and costly king, however, unless problems in its mining and use are solved. "There are two things wrong with coal," said S. David Freeman, director of an energy study for the Ford Foundation. "We can't mine it and we can't burn it."

Whether coal is mined underground or strip mined, damage to the environment can be severe. Wastes from underground mines pollute water, and the mines have also caused two million acres of land to settle and sink, breaking roads and sewers and making houses collapse. Strip mining pollutes streams and lakes, and mining companies have left millions of acres scarred and practically useless.

Some states require coal companies to restore the land somewhat, by replacing the overburden and by planting grasses and young trees. But these efforts cost money and reduce profits, so the companies do as little as possible and nothing at all in states where they aren't required to reclaim the land. Environmentalists have battled for years to establish a national law requiring reclamation of strip-mined land.

Coal from strip mines is cheaper than deep-mined coal, and the growing demand for coal will increase strip mining, especially in the West. An estimated 25 billion tons of coal lie in Colorado, Montana, Wyoming, Utah, New Mexico, and North Dakota. An area near the Wyoming–Montana border contains some of the richest coal deposits in the world, with beds of coal up to 150 feet thick, sometimes with an overburden of only a few feet.

In 1971 a group of electric utilities released plans for power generation from coal in Wyoming and Montana and other North Central states. The proposed North Central Power Project calls for 42 power plants in five states and thousands of miles of transmission lines to carry electricity to the Midwest.

The National Academy of Sciences has studied some of the possible environmental effects of strip mining in the North Central states. The Academy's 1973 report revealed that coal seams are natural storage areas for underground water (called groundwater). Removal of the coal will probably cause wells to go dry; even wells several miles away from mines may be affected. The loss of groundwater

Strip mining has scarred the landscape of Appalachia (above). In the photo below, sixty feet of overburden had to be removed in order to mine a coal seam in Montana.

will probably cause the death of plant life that provides food and shelter for wildlife and cattle and helps keep soil from washing away.

The scientists who prepared the Academy's report found that areas receiving more than ten inches of rain a year could be reclaimed and could once again support plants and animals. But none of these stripped areas could be restored to their former beauty or to their natural communities of plants and animals. Also, some of the western coal country receives less than ten inches of rain each year. The scientists warned that these desert and shrub lands, once strip-mined, might not support plant life again for centuries.

People have every reason to be concerned about the environmental effects of increased strip mining, especially in the North Central states. There are huge amounts of coal in the region. Inevitably, it will be used for energy. Unless the coal is mined and used with great care, however, there may be great and lasting damage to the land and its life.

Once out of the ground, coal presents a second problem: it is a filthy fuel. Like all fossil fuels, coal is a hydrocarbon—a mixture of carbon and hydrogen. It also contains varying amounts of water and other substances, and they affect the amount of energy the coal produces. They also make coal the dirtiest of all fossil fuels.

Sulfur is the most damaging pollutant in coal. Sulfur combines with oxygen when coal burns and forms sulfur oxides, which damage metals, crops, and people's lungs.

Anthracite is the top grade of coal. It contains very little sulfur. It also has high energy content because it contains more carbon and less water than other grades of coal. Anthracite yields as much as 16,000 British thermal units (Btu) per pound. (A British thermal unit is the amount of energy needed to raise the temperature of a pound of water one degree Fahrenheit.) However, anthracite is the least abundant kind of coal in America. Most coal reserves are either bituminous, subbituminous, or lignite. Bituminous coal contains high amounts of sulfur; the other two kinds of coal are relatively free of sulfur, but when burned they spew into the air large amounts of particles called fly ash. They also produce only about 5,500 to 8,000 Btu a pound.

Scientists are confident that the pollution problems of coal can be solved, but studies of coal-cleaning methods have lagged for many years. The Office of Coal Research, a division of the United States Bureau of Mines, received little money until the early 1970s. This neglect was probably caused in part by the oil industry. It has a powerful influence on government and has opposed research on other fuels. Energy shortages caused a long overdue increase in money for coal research. This may also have been helped by the movement of oil companies into the coal business. Some major coal companies have been bought by "oil giants," which now control about 20 percent of coal production.

Making coal a cleaner fuel is vital if it is to replace other fossil fuels. Each day more than a million barrels of oil are burned to produce electricity. If coal were to replace this

Studies by the Bureau of Mines are aimed at removing sulfur dioxide and fly ash from the "smoke stacks" of coal-burning power plants.

oil, the amounts of imported oil could be reduced, or the oil could be used in other ways.

Unfortunately, in recent years the trend has been for oil to replace coal. During the 1960s and early 1970s, about 400 utilities switched their power plants from coal to oil, or built new plants that burned only oil. One reason for this change was the increasingly strict air pollution laws. The state of New Jersey and the cities of New York and Boston, among others, set air quality standards allowing very little sulfur oxides to be released into the air. This means that fuel (either coal or oil) must have less than 1 percent sulfur.

Bituminous coal from eastern and midwestern states usually contains more than 3 percent sulfur. So the coal that is closest to the major cities of the Midwest and East has been outlawed. Power plants in Chicago have had to buy low-sulfur coal from as far away as Montana, even though high-sulfur coal can be mined in Illinois itself and in nearby states.

Fortunately, studies by the Bureau of Mines have led to the development of ways to remove most of the sulfur and fly ash from coal either before, during, or after burning. There are devices, called scrubbers, that remove sulfur oxides from the waste gases that go up "smoke stacks." Building better scrubbers has been a goal of the Bureau of Mines, and its engineers have made progress. Tests in a pilot plant located in Terre Haute, Indiana, showed that 95 percent of the sulfur oxides can be removed from stack gases.

The Bureau of Mines estimates that this method will cost about $4 a ton when used in a big power plant. At one time this additional charge would have made "clean" coal too expensive, but rising costs of petroleum products have changed that. Utilities in eastern and midwestern cities may find it cheaper to burn clean coal than imported oil. This change will have to wait, however, for the installation of modern stack gas scrubbers on power plants.

Coal can also be cleaned by a process called solvent refining. Under high temperature and pressure, coal is dissolved in a solvent that contains hydrogen. Once the coal is

Solvent refined coal process.

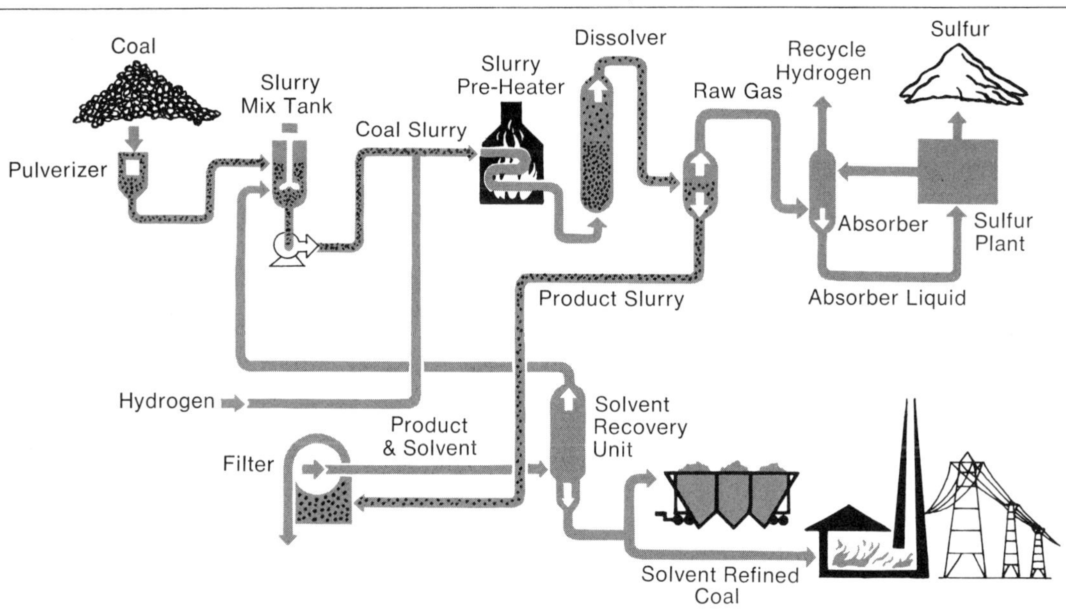

liquid, sulfur can be filtered from it. The solvent can also be recovered and used again. The process produces several useful byproducts besides sulfur, including benzene and oil. The refined coal is heavy, contains very little sulfur and ash, and has a high heating value of 16,000 Btu a pound. It can be piped as a liquid to a furnace and burned directly or cooled into a brittle solid and burned later.

The Office of Coal Research was aware of the solvent-refining process for several years before it was able to get enough federal funds to build a pilot plant. That plant, in Tacoma, Washington, was intended to give the process a real test, beginning in 1975.

Coal can also be changed to cleaner fuels by a process called pyrolysis. When coal is heated in a container without oxygen, it breaks down into charcoal, oil, and a low-Btu gas. A pilot plant demonstrating this process has been operating since 1970, but the coal and oil cost so much to produce that no company has been interested in building a large-scale plant. As prices of other fuels rise, however, the products of coal pyrolysis may seem more reasonable.

Scientists are also investigating ways of changing coal into a gas. Making gas from coal is not a new idea; coal gas was once a common source of heat and light in homes and factories. The gas produced then was at least half hydrogen, and its energy content (Btu) was low. In coal-gasification, water is heated to produce steam which reacts with the carbon in coal and forms a hydrogen-rich gas like methane. The process includes several steps which remove sulfur and other byproducts.

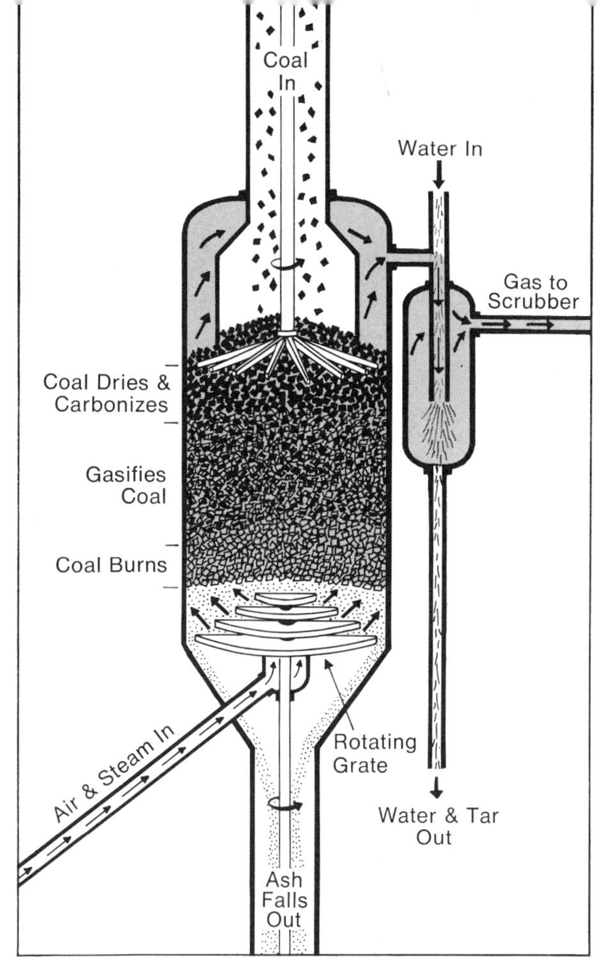

Lurgi coal-gasification.

Several new methods of coal-gasification are being tested in pilot plants. The aim is to produce a clean-burning fuel with the same heating quality of natural gas—about 1,000 Btu per cubic foot. Using high temperatures and pressures, they produce gas from coal that is mostly methane. However, these methods are still at the experimental stage, and large-scale production of high-Btu gas from coal is not expected until about 1985.

The only gasification process now used commercially produces coal gas with less than half the heating value of natural gas. Called the Lurgi process, it is used in Aus-

*A "mine mouth" power plant—
the Mohave Generating Station in Nevada.*

tralia, South Africa, and western Europe. Several gas companies in the United States plan to begin using the Lurgi process.

Another kind of coal gas, called power gas, produces 150 Btus per cubic foot. Power gas is cheaper to produce than high-Btu gas and, although it can't be used as a substitute for natural gas, it can be used as fuel in factories and utilities. Since power gas is not worth as much as natural gas, it is not economical to pipe long distances. But electric companies are investigating the idea of producing power gas right where coal is mined, burning it to produce electricity, then transmitting the electricity to cities. This is one kind of "mine mouth" power generation.

"Mine mouth" power generation from coal itself (not power gas) is already taking place. The best known generating station is the Four Corners Power Plant in northwestern New Mexico. Each day more than 22,000 tons of coal are strip-mined from a Navajo Indian reservation to fuel this power plant. The electricity is sent as far away as Los Angeles, California. At least a half-dozen similar plants are planned or already built in the Southwest.

The idea of *in situ* production of power gas is also being studied in Wyoming by the Bureau of Mines. Holes were drilled down 400 feet to a coal seam. After the coal was broken up by hydrofracturing, it was lit and was kept burning with the help of air forced down into the seam. The low-Btu gas piped to the surface contained large amounts of nitrogen and other impurities, but there are ways of removing these substances.

Another *in situ* coal-gasification project is planned for an eastern coal area near Morgantown, West Virginia. Bureau engineers believe that underground coal gasification may be the most practical way of getting energy from very deep or very thick coal seams, and from coal that contains a lot of ash. Many of the hazards and environmental problems of other mining methods would be avoided. However, at least two problems might remain: sinking land after gasification of the coal, and pollution of ground-water.

Despite problems in its mining and use, coal is a versatile and vital fuel. It can be used as a solid, liquid, or gas. Gasoline can be made from coal. The Germans did it during World War II, and the Office of Coal Research is testing the process in a West Virginia pilot plant. As petroleum prices rise, the high cost of making gasoline from coal may become more reasonable.

Coal can also be made into methanol, a product that may help extend present gasoline supplies. Methanol is sometimes called methyl alcohol or wood alcohol. Most people know it as Sterno, the fuel used to heat food at the table. It can be made from natural gas, petroleum, coal, wood, garbage, and farm wastes.

Engineers working at the Massachusetts Institute of Technology found that methanol mixed with gasoline has several good effects on automobiles: they use less fuel, produce less pollution, and accelerate faster. The engineers concluded that "if gasoline becomes scarce or too expensive, we can design cars that will operate on pure methanol and cause less pollution."

Methanol is also a safe, clean fuel for home heating or for electricity generation. It was too expensive in the past to compete with petroleum products, even with the advantages of its cleanliness. Once again, rising costs of petroleum may change that. In the past most methanol was made from natural gas, but the large amounts needed in the future will probably come from coal—and in the more distant future, from wood and garbage.

Whether coal is burned directly or changed to other fuels, the United States will depend on it more and more. We are lucky in having enough coal to last 500 years at the rate it was being used in the early 1970s. Remember, though, that the coal consumed then provided only about 18 percent of the nation's energy. As coal fills increasing amounts of our energy needs, coal reserves will be used up much more rapidly. The change from petroleum and natural gas to coal will not be easy and will not be cheap. The difficulties of that change should not keep us from facing an even greater task: finding energy to use after all fossil fuels are gone.

ENERGY FROM ATOMS

The "peaceful atom" provided less than 2 percent of the energy used in the United States in 1973. After a slow start, however, the nuclear energy industry is developing rapidly. A total of 42 nuclear power plants were operating or ready to operate at the end of 1973. Fifty-six more plants were being built, and more than a hundred others had been ordered. If nuclear power develops as predicted, it will provide 20 percent of the United States' electricity by 1980. People in some areas already depend heavily on nuclear power. In 1974 a third of the electricity produced by Commonwealth Edison in Illinois came from seven nuclear plants.

The nuclear power industry has advertised its product as "clean energy," and in some ways it is much cleaner than fossil fuels. No fly ash or sulfur oxides are given off by nuclear power plants. But there is not yet any plentiful source of truly clean energy—only a choice of poisons. And nuclear energy is considered to be the most hazardous of all energy sources.

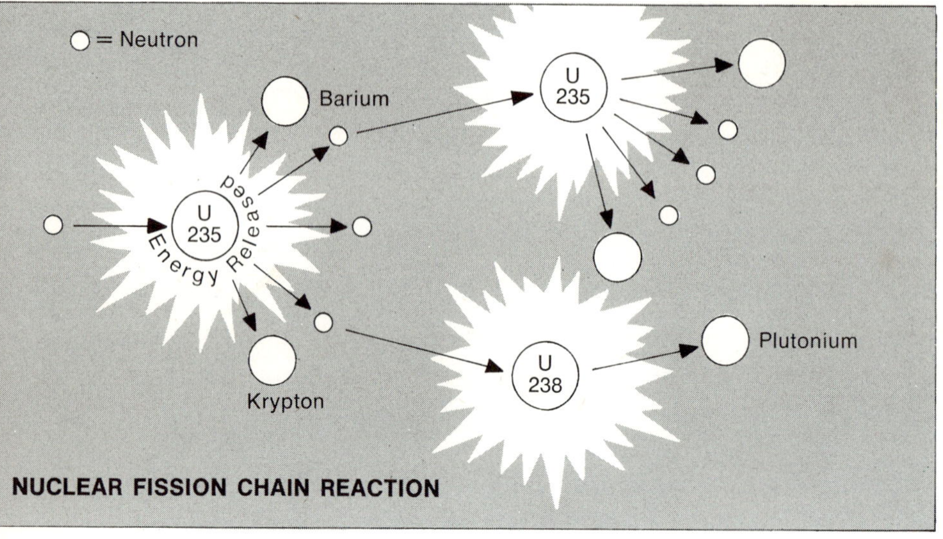

When a neutron strikes a uranium-235 atom, the atom splits and gives off energy and three neutrons.

Nuclear power plants produce heat energy by splitting atoms of elements like uranium. The atom-splitting process is called fission. A single half-ounce pellet of uranium oxide, about the size of a thimble, releases as much energy as 160 gallons of oil. All of the commercial nuclear plants being built in the United States use this process. These power plants use the heat energy from fission to boil water, producing steam to drive electric generators.

But the fission process has many drawbacks. First of all, it is very inefficient. Nuclear power plants, or reactors, "burn" a rare kind of uranium called U-235 and cannot make energy from the more abundant form of uranium, U-238. At the rate fission reactors are using U-235, most of the United States' supply of high-grade uranium may be used up in the next few decades.

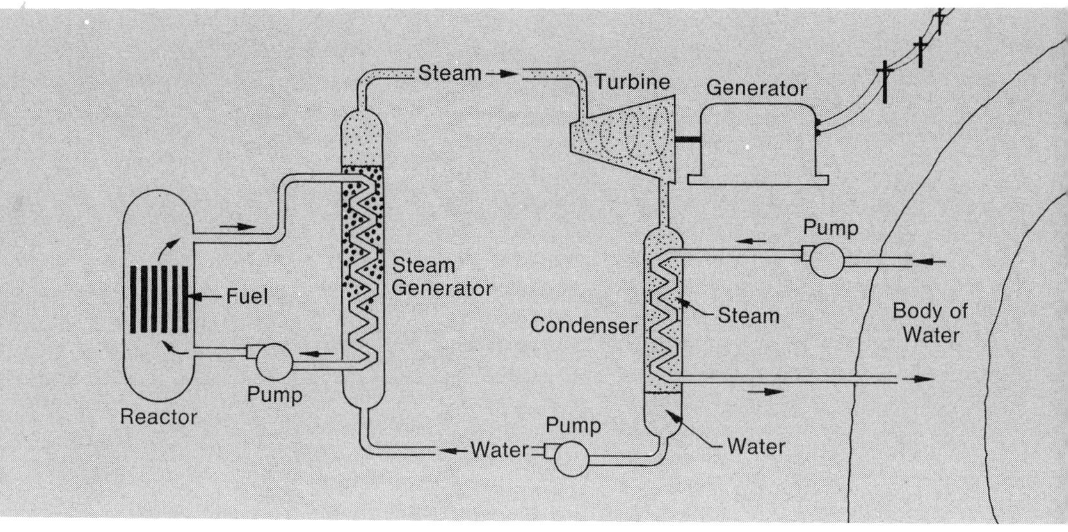

A simplified view of a nuclear electric plant.

Fission reactors now in use are inefficient in another way. They convert only about 32 percent of the energy produced into electricity. The rest of the heat energy produced in the fission process is wasted. As the reactors are water-cooled, they produce tremendous quantities of hot water. Most nuclear power plants dump this water directly into rivers and lakes—sometimes at the rate of 850,000 gallons a minute.

Waste heat is usually called thermal pollution. It can have several bad effects on fish: killing them directly, preventing their eggs from hatching, or stimulating the growth of disease organisms. In northern states, the warm water attracts fish in winter. This can lead to disaster for the fish, as schools of them are sucked into a power plant along with its cooling water.

Another kind of disaster may happen when a power plant stops operating. In 1973 and 1974, a New Jersey nuclear reactor shut down briefly in February and thousands of fish died in a nearby bay. Normally the fish would have swum to warmer southern waters before winter came. Instead, they stayed near the power plant, and died when the flow of warm water stopped.

According to some estimates, one-third of all the water flowing in the United States will be needed to cool power plants (nuclear and fossil-fuel) by the end of this century. Some practical but small-scale uses for waste heat have been discovered, and there is hope that power plants can be made less wasteful. Nuclear reactors cooled with helium gas, for example, are more efficient than those cooled by water. But most of the nuclear power plants now operating or planned are water-cooled. In some states, electric utilities are required by law to build cooling towers, which release waste heat into the air and not into streams and lakes.

Serious though it is, waste heat is a minor problem when compared with other wastes of the fission process. When an atom of uranium breaks up, it emits particles which cannot be seen or felt but which can harm living things. In humans, exposure to radiation can cause leukemia and other kinds of cancer. It can damage genes, which determine the characteristics that parents pass on to their children. So people are understandably concerned about radioactivity given off by reactors, by wastes from reactors, and by plutonium, a byproduct of fission.

Cooling towers like these, up to 500 feet tall, may become a common sight near electric power plants.

Worn-out nuclear power equipment being buried near Richland, Washington. Radioactive nuclear wastes are even more difficult to dispose of.

During the 1960s and 1970s people became increasingly critical of the Atomic Energy Commission (AEC), which had the dual role of regulating the nuclear power industry and promoting the growth of nuclear power. Finally, in 1975 the AEC was dissolved and its responsibilities divided between the Nuclear Regulatory Commission (NRC) and the Energy Research and Development Administration (ERDA). However, this did not end concern about release of radioactivity, or other problems of nuclear energy production.

The increasing numbers of nuclear plants will worsen another problem: what to do with radioactive wastes from reactors. The wastes are shipped to fuel reprocessing plants where some uranium and plutonium are reclaimed for later use as fuel. One kind of waste, a radioactive gas called krypton-85, is released into the air. The remaining solid and liquid wastes are highly radioactive. Some remain dangerous for hundreds of years, others for thousands of years, and plutonium for hundreds of thousands of years.

About 100 million gallons of nuclear wastes are now stored temporarily in steel and concrete tanks. The volume of these wastes will increase greatly in the years ahead. The AEC hoped to "dispose" of radioactive wastes by placing them in strong ceramic containers and burying them in deep, thick salt deposits. But the first site chosen, in Kansas, was abandoned when the AEC discovered that many exploratory oil and gas wells had been drilled nearby. These uncharted wells might have allowed radiation to escape to the surface. The NRC is investigating other sites but so far this great and growing problem of nuclear wastes has no solution. Speaking of these wastes, Dr. David J. Rose, a nuclear engineer at the Massachusetts Institute of Technology, said, "If society wants nuclear power, it must be prepared to undertake a perpetual care problem, and build better than the pyramids."

Nuclear reactors pose another safety problem: the possibility of an accident in which radioactive materials would spew out for miles around. The most likely kind of accident, according to nuclear engineers, is called LOCA, which stands for Loss-Of-Coolant Accident. If a reactor's supply of cooling water was suddenly lost—through faulty construction, sabotage, or an earthquake or other natural disaster—the fission process could be slowed down but not stopped immediately. Great amounts of heat would be released by some of the fission products, and the core of fuel might melt right through the bottom of the power plant and into the earth. It would stay radioactive for many years. As serious as this would be, the most worrisome part of a LOCA would take place in the first hour or so, as radioactive gases and particles spread through the air. The effect on living things might be like that of dropping an atomic bomb.

The AEC and its successor, the NRC, devised safeguards against accidents, including emergency cooling systems. Many nuclear scientists believe that the chances of a reactor accident of any kind are very small. Others, including several scientists who worked for the AEC, NRC, or the nuclear power industry, are not so confident.

If nuclear development expands, greater amounts of

radioactive fuel and wastes will be shipped about the United States and the world. This will increase the chances for serious accidents, and for the theft of plutonium. Just a few pounds are needed to make a crude nuclear bomb. Information for building such a bomb is readily available, and terrible weapons can be made by a small group of people or, perhaps, by one person working alone. Many people consider this the most serious of all problems related to nuclear power. Unfortunately, all these problems will be made worse by the next stage of nuclear development—the breeder reactor.

The world's first breeder reactor began operating in 1951, in Idaho. It was a small, experimental device, but it produced the first electric power from nuclear energy. An attempt to operate a commercial breeder reactor failed in 1966. A demonstration breeder plant is to be built in Tennessee and may be operating by the mid-1980's.

Other nations are further along in development of breeder reactors. Full-scale commercial breeders began operating in France and the Soviet Union in 1973, and similar reactors were then nearly ready in Scotland and West Germany. However, only the United States seems committed to rapid commercial development of breeders.

The United States has invested huge amounts of money in breeder research. The "liquid metal fast breeder reactor"—its official name—is the nation's most costly energy research project. It has one big advantage over present fission plants in that it converts more of the abundant uranium-238 to plutonium. In this way the reactor produces more fuel than it uses, and this is why it is called a "breeder." (It is called a "fast" breeder because of the speed at which neutrons travel within the reactor.) Breeder reactors can also produce nuclear fuel from thorium, an element which is about as plentiful as uranium in the United States. Breeder reactors could stretch nuclear fuel supplies far into the future. They also are expected to operate more efficiently than present reactors.

Because of the great heat produced by fission in breeders, liquid sodium may be used as the coolant in some breeders. It boils at far higher temperatures than water. Each second, several tons of sodium will be pumped through the reactor, carrying heat away from it. The sodium will become highly radioactive, so the heat will be transferred to another flow of sodium, which will deliver the heat to water in boilers. Steam from the boilers will drive the turbines which produce electricity.

Breeders have been called "our best hope today for meeting the nation's growing demand for economical clean power." On the other hand, some people say that breeders ought to be "the last choice of a desperate nation." Breeders represent the same hazards as fission plants, and may be much more dangerous.

The AEC estimated that as many as 500 breeder reactors would be operating in the United States by the year 2000. In contrast, ERDA's 1975 plans for energy development foresaw no significant amounts of power from breeders in this century. Opposition to breeders increased, partly because of the great amounts of plutonium that would be produced

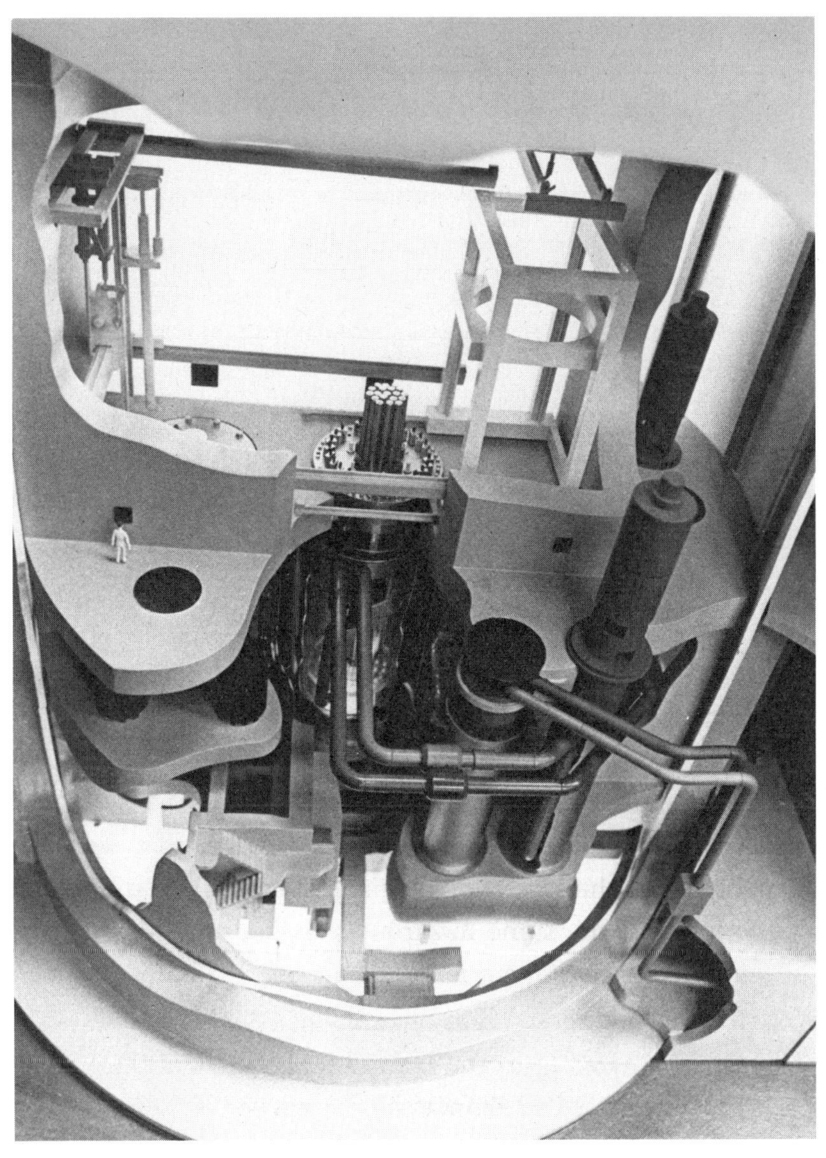

A model of a liquid metal fast breeder nuclear reactor.

by these reactors. Plutonium is one of the most poisonous substances known. It loses its radioactivity very slowly, with only half of it gone after 24,400 years. An area would be uninhabitable for much longer than that if there was an accidental spill of plutonium or a major accident at a breeder reactor.

Because of their complex design and higher operating temperatures, breeders need even greater safeguards than present reactors. A growing number of scientists believe that much more research is needed on breeders before any attempt is made to start large-scale commercial development. The need for hasty development of breeders was questioned in a 1974 study by physicist Thomas B. Cochran. He found evidence that United States uranium reserves are much greater than estimated by the AEC. If this is true, there is more time available to thoroughly investigate *all* alternatives to the present reactors.

The United States has spent small amounts of money studying other kinds of breeder reactors. A gas-cooled reactor, for example, might have some advantages over reactors cooled by liquid sodium. The coolant would be helium gas. It does not become radioactive as sodium does. It could be used to drive turbines directly, rather than heating water to make steam. Helium also has some disadvantages as a coolant, but many nuclear scientists hope that more attention and money will be aimed at developing gas-cooled reactors. However, by 1976 the future of the breeder reactor and of all nuclear development was in doubt. Public concern continued to grow, and rising costs of nuclear power plants caused many utilities to cancel orders for reactors. It appeared that the cost advantage of nuclear power was vanishing, and electricity from nuclear power plants would soon be more expensive than from coal-fired plants.

The lack of national energy planning has been costly. The United States put nearly all of its energy research eggs in one nuclear "basket." (The amount of money spent on nuclear fission studies every year, for example, has been at least a hundred times the amount spent on coal-gasification studies.) This mistake was compounded by focusing nearly all of our long-range nuclear research efforts on fission in sodium-cooled breeders. As a result, we know very little about other, less hazardous sources of energy. Or, as S. David Freeman said at a 1972 energy conference: "The whole future of our high energy civilization is hanging on a very thin thread indeed."

One possible alternative to breeder reactors is nuclear fusion. It operates on a large scale in the universe, powering all of the stars, including our sun. Humans first developed fusion in hydrogen bombs. For a while during the 1950s, scientists were optimistic about rapid development of fusion power. But progress was slow. Hopes have risen again during the past few years. Many scientists think that the fusion process can be controlled and produce electricity economically by 1980. But large-scale development is not expected until 1990 at the earliest.

In fission, heavy atoms (uranium, plutonium) release energy as they split apart. In fusion, light atoms (hydrogen) give off energy as they are forced together, or fused.

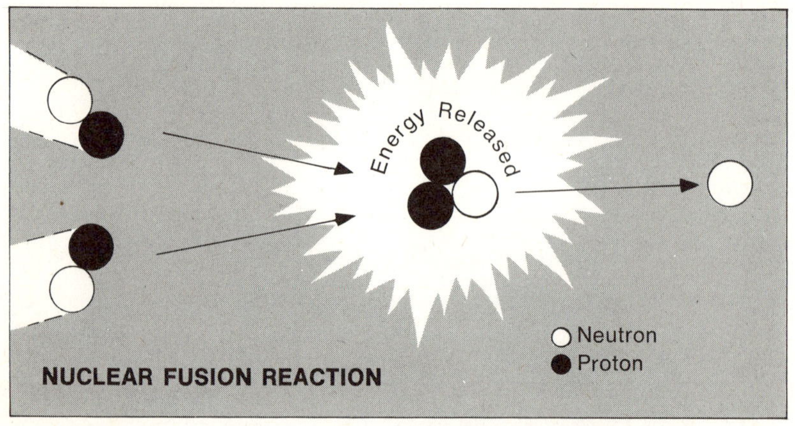

When deuterium and tritium fuse to form the nucleus of a helium atom, energy and a neutron are released.

The likely fuels for controlled fusion are two forms of the element hydrogen. One is tritium, which can be made from lithium, an abundant element. The other is deuterium, which is found naturally in seawater. There is enough deuterium in 264 gallons of seawater to produce more than 400,000 kilowatt-hours of electricity.

That is one great advantage of fusion power—the fuel supplies are abundant enough to last for millions of years. There are other advantages as well. A fusion plant would probably be very efficient, converting as much as 60 percent of its heat energy to electricity and releasing much less waste heat than a fission plant. Big shipments of radioactive fuels would not be necessary for fusion reactors. The reactors themselves would produce no fusion products that would need long storage. Fusion seems almost too good to be true—and it may be. The "pure" fusion reactor described above has not been built, and may never be built.

In this model of a Tokomak-type fusion device, a cutaway view shows the coils which produce a "magnetic bottle" to contain the nuclear fuel.

The greatest known disadvantage of fusion reactors would be release of tritium. It is a light gas that spreads rapidly and is very difficult to contain. Tritium is radioactive but not nearly as dangerous or as long-lasting as the wastes of fission. Controlling the leakage of tritium is one of many fusion problems that remain to be solved.

The fusion reaction takes place at incredibly high temperatures—more than 200 million°F (111 million°C). The temperatures are so high that no metal or other substance can contain the fuel without melting. Also, the fusion process stops if the fuel touches the walls of a container. So the process goes on in a "magnetic bottle," where strong magnetic fields hold the nuclear fuel inside a chamber and keep it from touching the walls.

So far experimental fusion reactors have produced less energy than the electricity needed to create the magnetic field. A Soviet fusion device called Tokomak seems most promising, and scientists in several nations are working with Tokomak-type reactors. Meanwhile, other approaches to fusion power are being investigated.

In 1968 Soviet scientists discovered that a high-powered laser could start a fusion reaction. Some scientists expect that the feasibility of laser fusion will be proved in a few years. Others, looking at the painfully slow progress of fusion research so far, are less optimistic.

Laser fusion is dramatically different from fusion confined by magnetic forces. A small pellet of deuterium and tritium is fired into a reactor. There it is struck by many laser beams from different directions. In a tiny fraction of a second, the pellet heats to fusion temperature and gives off

Progress in laser research will affect the pace of nuclear fusion development.

a pulse of energy. Because of the great pressure on the pellet caused by the lasers, and because of the speed of the reaction, the fuel does not expand much. This makes it possible for the reactor walls to withstand the heat and explosion of energy.

A laser fusion power plant might "burn" a hundred pellets a second. It would produce far less radioactive tritium than magnetically controlled fusion. Laser fusion reactors might also be made small enough to power ships and factories. In the mid-1970s, however, laser fusion seemed a long way from the power plant stage. The amount of energy used by lasers in experiments was greater than the nuclear energy produced. But nuclear scientists expect that stronger lasers, once developed, will eventually help release the fantastic amounts of energy available in deuterium.

Studies of laser fusion led scientists to yet another idea for producing power from nuclear fuel. The fuel would be a pellet with a core of deuterium and tritium and a coating of boron. Lasers would cause the fusion of the two core elements. The energy from that reaction would trigger the fission of the boron. The process would be highly efficient and would yield very little radioactive waste. Like the basic laser fusion process, however, this method awaits the development of more powerful lasers.

The long-term prospects of getting abundant and perhaps even clean energy from nuclear reactions seem good. But for now, the nuclear power available has potential side effects that, if uncontrolled, could bring disaster.

CLEANER, SAFER FUELS

HYDROELECTRIC POWER

In 1974 about 4 percent of our energy came from water power—hydroelectric dams built on rivers. Water power is not expected to increase much in the future, however, because most of the best dam sites in North America have been developed. In other nations though, this cheap and clean source of energy can be developed much further. Worldwide, less than 10 percent of the hydroelectric potential is being used.

Another kind of water power comes from tides, which are caused by the pull of the moon's gravity. Along some coasts, a bay can be dammed so that the power of incoming and outgoing water is converted to electricity. Two modern tidal power plants have been built, in France and the Soviet Union. Tidal power is not as cheap as hydroelectric power because it costs much more to build a tidal plant than a dam. It is not nearly as plentiful either. Tidal power may eventually provide electricity for some coastal areas which have the right conditions for development of this resource.

A tidal power plant, at the mouth of the Rance River, France.

Both tidal and hydroelectric power are alike in one important way: they are renewable resources. They are available as long as the moon is the earth's satellite, and as long as the sun shines—since it is energy from the sun that powers the earth's water cycle and thus keeps rivers flowing and energy from the moon's gravitational pull that produces tides. There are other renewable energy sources, including the sun, the winds, and perhaps heat from the earth. Probably none will produce much power for human use soon, but scientists are confident that these great sources of energy can be tapped.

GEOTHERMAL POWER

Long ago, when people found oil and tar in pools, they believed that these seepage areas were the earth's only supplies of petroleum. In the same way, people have considered geysers, volcanoes, and hot springs the only sources of geothermal energy. We now know that there are vast underground supplies of heat that can be converted to electricity. Dr. Joseph Barnea, an energy expert formerly at the United Nations, says, "We have geothermal energy in practically every geological environment, whereas petroleum is restricted to sedimentary areas of the world. In 50 years, geothermal energy will be recognized as an energy source of even greater significance than petroleum."

Geothermal heat is a kind of "fossil nuclear energy." It is caused by the decay of radioactive materials deep inside the earth. The heat produced is so great that parts of the

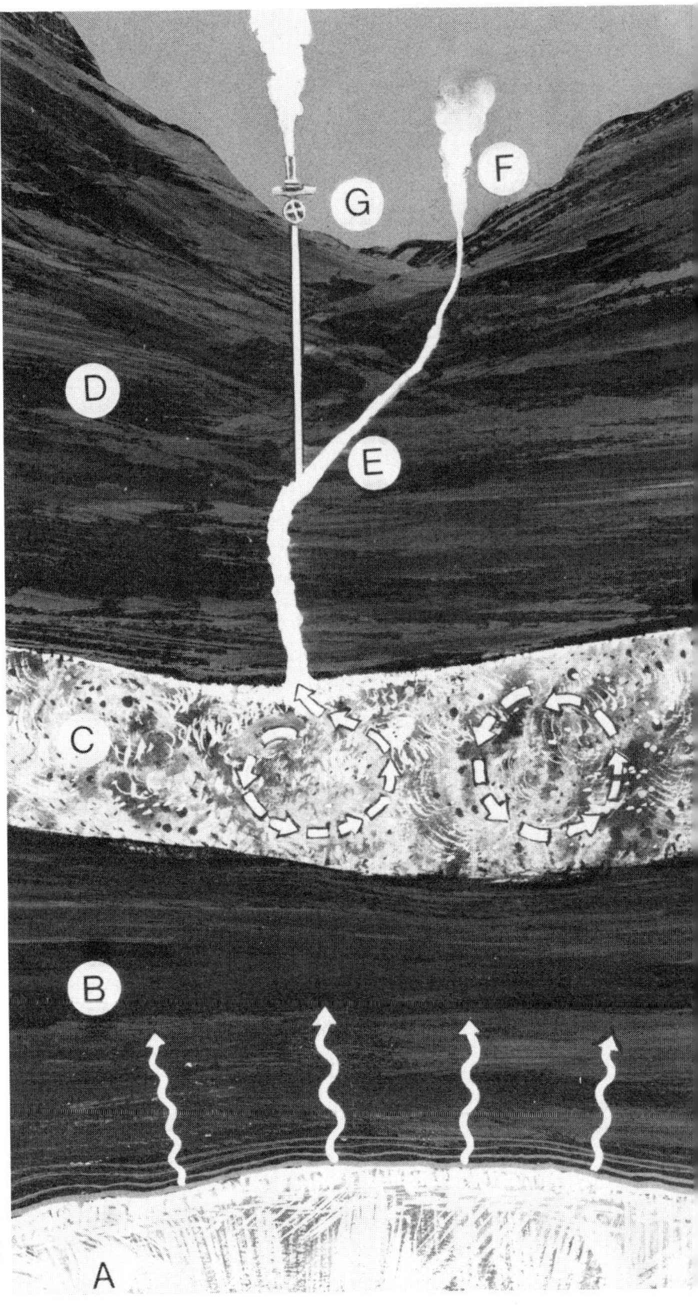

In areas where molten rock (A) is close to the earth's surface, heat passes upward through solid rock (B) and boils water within porous rock (C). Steam is unable to pass through solid rock (D), but does reach the surface through fissures (E) which lead to geysers, fumaroles, or hot springs (F). The steam can also be tapped by geothermal wells (G).

Part of the Geysers geothermal power plant, in northern California.

earth are liquid—molten rock or magma. This molten rock sometimes reaches the surface, as active volcanoes, and is close to the surface in other areas. But heat from the earth affects all of the earth's crust; the temperature rises about 2°F (about 1°C) for every hundred feet beneath the surface. However, the most likely sources of power from geothermal heat are the "hot spots"—underground reservoirs where heat has built up and is stored in the form of steam and hot water.

Electricity from geothermal heat was first produced in 1904, when steam from underground was used at Larderello, Italy. Today the same area is still in use, producing about 400,000 kilowatts of electricity a year. Electric power is also produced commercially from geothermal energy in seven other countries, including New Zealand, Japan, and the Soviet Union. Geothermal heat is also used directly, to warm buildings, in the city of Reykjavík, Iceland. Many other nations are investigating geothermal energy. It may be especially valuable to poor nations in Central America and East Africa which lack fossil fuels.

Since 1960 geothermal steam has provided some power for the Pacific Gas and Electric Company in northern California. The steam is easily tapped at an area called the Geysers. Complete development of the area is expected in 1977; at that time the steam will generate enough electricity to supply the needs of a city the size of San Francisco.

The Geysers and the Larderello area in Italy produce "dry" steam, without a flow of hot water. This helps make power generation easy and cheap. Construction and maintenance costs are much lower than those for fossil fuel or nuclear plants. But sources of dry steam are rare. Most "hot spots" produce small amounts of steam and large amounts of hot water. Even after it is separated from the steam, the hot water causes problems.

Usually the hot water contains salts and other minerals. Because of its minerals and heat, the water cannot be dumped into nearby streams. The minerals also corrode and clog pipes, turbines, and drilling equipment. Difficulties caused by mineral-laden water have slowed the development of the greatest known source of geothermal energy—the Imperial Valley of southern California.

There is great potential energy beneath the Imperial Valley, but studies there reveal some of the problems that may slow geothermal development everywhere. Seven wells were drilled in the valley and brought forth jets of steam and brine, at temperatures up to 700°F (371°C). But the salt and other minerals quickly damaged turbines and other equipment and work was halted.

The companies that are trying to tap the valley's geothermal power will test another method—using the steam to heat isobutane gas, which can be used to drive turbines which then generate electricity. The hot water will not be used; it will be put back into the ground. If the steam alone causes serious corrosion of pipes and other equipment, the project may have to be abandoned for a while—until metals or mixtures of metals are found that will withstand the corrosive minerals. A company official said, "We may have to wait for technology to catch up with our problems."

One of the attractions of the geothermal resources in southern California and in other dry western areas is the water itself. The water could be desalted cheaply, since it is already hot and the greatest expense in desalting water is heating it. Scientists estimate that a full-scale Imperial Valley geothermal project could produce 5 million to 7 million acre-feet of fresh water annually. (An acre-foot is the amount of water needed to cover an acre one foot deep.) But questions have been raised about the reliability of this water supply.

How long will it last? For that matter, how long will a geothermal field go on producing energy? Some evidence comes from Larderello, Italy, where geothermal power production has gone on the longest. Wells there have constant output of steam for about ten years. Then more wells must be drilled to keep production steady. Over the years the steam has become drier and hotter. It seems that the underground water supply is running out.

Geologists can only make rough estimates of the speed with which underground water is replaced in geothermal fields. Tests of water from some wells in the Imperial Valley seem to show that the water there is thousands of years old. This suggests that it is replenished very slowly. At the Geysers, it is considered wise to put some water back into the earth. Unused steam is cooled in cooling towers, and the water that condenses from the steam is injected into deep wells. This also may help avoid the problem of sinking land, which occurs above some oil fields after years of production.

However, no one knows the effects of large-scale injection of water into a geothermal field. It could cause earthquakes and might not keep the land from sinking, because the injected water would be concentrated in a few areas until it gradually spread through the rocks below.

So far, most research of geothermal energy has been aimed at "hot spots" like the Imperial Valley, where a combination of water and nearby magma produce great amounts of steam and hot water. But it is more common to find areas of deep rock that are free of water. Scientists are investigating one way of getting energy from these areas. In 1973 the first test of this method was conducted at the Los Alamos Scientific Laboratory in northern New Mexico.

A well was drilled about a half-mile into the rock. Then water was pumped under pressure into the lower section of the well in order to open cracks in the rock surrounding the well. The rocks fractured more easily than expected. The scientists were also pleased to discover that the cracks in the rock did not grow with time, or let water escape. Encouraged, the scientists will drill other, deeper wells and then set up and test a geothermal power system. It works like this:

After a well is drilled into dry, hot rock and an area of rock is hydrofractured, a second well is drilled 20 to 30 feet from the first. Water is pumped down the first hole. It flows through the cracked rock, taking heat from it, and then steam and hot water rise up the second well. They can be used to drive turbines directly, or indirectly by transferring their heat to isobutane. Once the system is started,

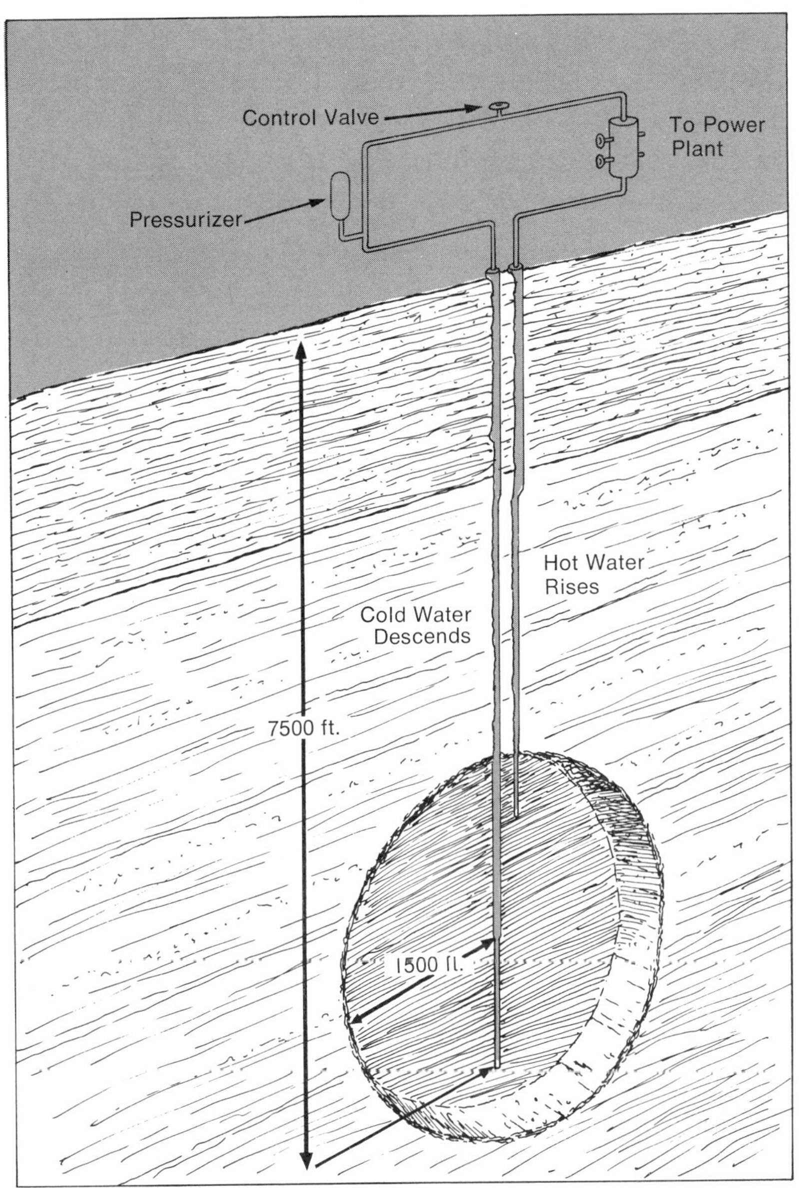

A geothermal power system in hot, dry rock.

pumping will probably not be needed, as the great difference in water temperatures keeps it flowing.

If this method of tapping geothermal energy is successful, it can be used almost anywhere on earth. At an energy conference in New York City, a scientist suggested that the city could heat its buildings by drilling 20,000 feet into the rocks below.

Energy from geothermal sources is clean, compared with nuclear and fossil fuels, but there are still some environmental problems. Besides salt, geothermal water and steam may contain sulfur, boron, ammonia, and other substances which can harm life if they are released into the air or streams. The cooling towers at the Geysers give off sulfur compounds into the air. The amount of sulfur released is about equal to that given off by a power plant of the same size burning low-sulfur oil. In some hot water areas, such as the Imperial Valley, greater amounts of sulfur compounds are expected.

"Scrubbing" devices may have to be developed in order to capture sulfur and other pollutants. Heat and water will be released into the air from cooling towers, of course, and may affect the climate near geothermal fields. These are some of the known environmental problems of geothermal energy. Others may be discovered through testing and small-scale development of hot water and hot rock.

Many scientists are optimistic about generating power from the earth's heat, though estimates of the importance of geothermal energy vary a lot. Some experts say it will become a major power source, perhaps replacing nuclear energy. Others say it will probably provide no more than 10 percent of the energy needs of the United States.

SOLAR POWER

Although there is great untapped power in the earth's heat, this energy is dwarfed by another undeveloped resource, the sun. We already depend on the sun's energy in some obvious ways. It heats the earth. It gives us all of our food, since solar energy is captured by green plants and converted to food on which all animals depend. Some of the sun's effects are less well-known. It powers the wind and the ocean currents—both of which may someday yield energy for people's use.

We use a lot of solar energy, but most of it indirectly. The heat from wood burned in stoves and fireplaces is really solar energy that was captured and stored by trees. And the energy of fossil fuels came from the sun, since all of these fuels began as organic (once-living) materials. There are other ways of using solar energy indirectly. Within the past few years, however, scientists have renewed their hopes that the sun's rays can be used directly to give people an almost never-ending source of clean energy.

There is plenty of solar energy available. Enough sunlight falls on the United States in just two days to provide more power than the country's known reserves of fossil fuels. The energy arrives, day after day. The challenges are to capture it, concentrate it, and store it.

Solar One, an experimental house at the University of Delaware, which uses solar energy for heating, cooling, and generating electricity to run appliances.

Development of solar energy would be further along if more money had been spent on research. So far, less than 1 percent of federal energy research funds have been spent on solar power. "The development of solar energy has lagged," explained one scientist, "because the oil companies don't own the sun."

Commercial use of solar energy is closer than most people realize. Many scientists believe that before 1980, people will be able to buy solar heating and cooling systems for homes at prices that are competitive with present methods. There are already thousands of small solar-powered water heaters in use, with an estimated 400,000 in Japan. Roughly 40 buildings in the world are heated by the sun. This number is expected to rise rapidly. In 1974, the National Science Foundation equipped four public schools with experimental solar systems designed to provide 40 percent of heating needs. Several office buildings in the Northeast have been designed for solar heating. If efforts like this are successful, many more people will become aware of the possibilities of solar energy.

For homes and other buildings, solar energy collectors are usually made of black metal, covered with one to three panes of glass which reduce heat loss. Water or air circulates through the heat collectors and carries heat throughout the building. Some of the heat can be stored (in water, chemicals, or rocks) for use at night or on cloudy days. Most solar homes also have a backup heating system. Scientists are experimenting with several different kinds of solar-powered air conditioners, but quite a few problems

Solar energy collectors outside a school in suburban Minneapolis.

must be solved before any solar air conditioning system is ready for commercial development.

In the past, solar heating systems were about twice as expensive to operate as oil or gas furnaces. But rising costs of fossil fuels have made solar units more competitive. Presently more than 20 percent of all energy consumed in the United States is used for heating or cooling homes and other buildings. Rapid acceptance of solar heating could ease shortages of fossil fuels. About half of the homes in western states are heated by natural gas, and many of these states also have abundant sunshine. Solar heating systems

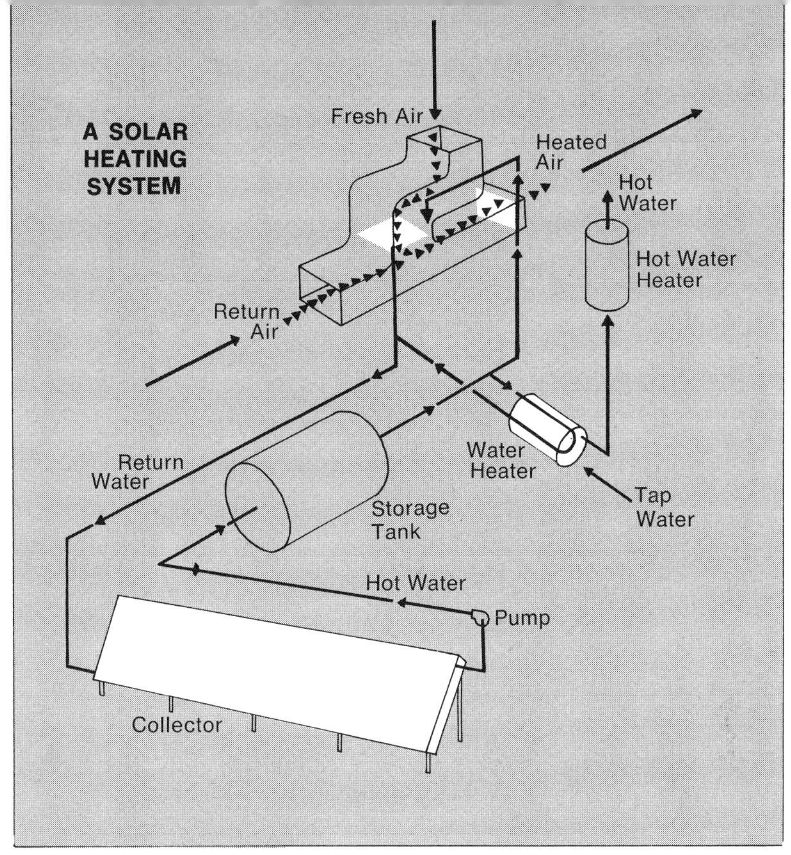

Solar energy heats water to 130°–150°F. The hot water is used directly in sinks and showers, or indirectly to heat the building.

would work especially well in these areas, and help reduce the demand for natural gas.

Widespread use of solar energy for heating seems close at hand; making great amounts of electricity from sunlight is farther away. There are two basic ways of changing sunlight to electricity. One is to use sunlight to heat water, with steam from the water then used to generate electricity. Modern steam turbines produce electricity when steam temperatures are between 300–600°F (149–316°C), so enough solar energy must be collected in order to heat water or another substance to those temperatures. Special mirrors or lenses may be needed to concentrate the sun's rays on heat collectors spread over a wide area.

Once the heat is collected, ways must be found to pipe it to turbines or to a storage container. The pipe must be specially designed to avoid losing much of the heat. Studies of piping systems and of different coatings for collectors will probably take many years and great sums of money before efficient and economical methods are found.

Another way of changing sunlight into electricity is to use solar cells, which are also called photovoltaic cells. They are the main source of power in space satellites. Solar cells are made of crystals of either silicon, cadmium sulfide, or gallium arsenide. The crystals produce an electric current when sunlight strikes them.

The major barrier to development of power plants using solar cells is the cost of making the cells. The raw materials are expensive, and manufacture of the crystals is slow, painstaking work. Cadmium sulfide crystals can be mass-produced, but they are less efficient than the other materials. They convert only 6 percent of the sunlight they receive into electricity. Cadmium sulfide cells also break down more quickly than other solar cell crystals.

In the early 1970s the cost of making solar cells was so great that scientists estimated it would have to be reduced a hundred times before cells could be used to produce power economically. Yet it seems likely that this will be accomplished. Rising interest in solar energy has loosed a flood of ideas. There are many problems yet to be solved, including the storage of electricity once it is produced by

An artist's view of a solar power station in space, sending energy to earth via microwaves.

solar cells. But the growing interest in solar energy, plus increasing amounts of money for research, will speed the solution of these problems.

The most "far out" idea for capturing solar energy was suggested by Dr. Peter Glaser of the research company Arthur D. Little, Inc. He suggests that one or more space power stations be put into orbit around the earth. Huge panels of solar cells on these satellites would collect sunlight and convert it to electricity. Each satellite would have a giant antenna which would then convert the electricity to microwaves which could be beamed to receiving antennae on earth. There the microwave beams would be changed to electricity once again.

This system would have one big advantage over solar power plants on earth. It would work day and night, eliminating the need for energy storage. The system also has some drawbacks, beginning with great cost. The microwave receiving antennae for one satellite would cover an area of about six square miles. Nothing could live in this area.

Although solar energy is "clean," compared with energy from nuclear or fossil fuels, its development may have some bad effects on the environment. The amount of sun energy falling on an acre of land or water is rather small. In order to collect great amounts of solar energy, many square miles of land or water will have to be covered with solar cells or other collecting devices. Of course, the surface may not be a solid mass of sunlight collectors. Perhaps livestock can be raised in between strips of collectors. On the other hand, waste heat from the collecting system might make the area too hot for farming or any other use.

Solar fuel is free, so only the great cost of solar energy devices prevents rapid development of this resource. Most research is aimed at eventually producing large amounts of power for industrial nations. But the development of cheap, small solar power machines also needs attention. They could be used for cooking, heating, water-pumping, and water-purifying in poor nations.

Solar energy collectors may someday cover vast areas of desert.

WIND POWER

People have been using wind energy for centuries. The oldest and most widespread use of wind power was sailing ships. Fossil fuels replaced the wind; now wind may replace fossil fuels. A German shipbuilder is working on a modern four-masted clipper ship which is expected to be as fast and reliable as ships powered by fossil fuels. The "Dyna-Ship" will have engines but will use them only in harbors and at windless times. The ship's designer estimates that it will use only 5 percent of the fossil fuels needed by a freighter.

On land, windmills have been used to pump water and turn millstones since the twelfth century. Windmills were first used to generate electricity in 1890. Their spinning blades were once a familiar sight in rural America. Windmills may become a common sight again. By the year 2000, wind power could produce 1.5 trillion kilowatt-hours of electricity in America, according to a study made by the National Science Foundation and the National Aeronautics and Space Administration (NASA). That is equal to all of the electricity used in the United States in 1970.

In the early 1940s electricity was made from a windmill built in the mountains of central Vermont. It produced less energy than expected, and was abandoned when one of the 65-foot blades broke. Since then there has been further

Windmills may once again be a common sight in North America, though many new designs are being studied.

A modern turbine used for wind power studies in Denmark.

This inexpensive windmill powers a water pump. It is made from two oil drums cut in half lengthwise and welded together to form troughs that catch the air.

study of wind power, the design and manufacture of blades have improved, and several wind turbines, as they are now called, are generating electricity in European countries.

The most successful of these turbines is in Denmark. It has three 40-foot blades mounted on a 75-foot concrete tower, and generates about 400,000 kilowatt hours a year. Danish engineers are optimistic about wind power development in their country. Coal and oil are scarce there, and the strongest winds occur in winter, when the demand for electricity is greatest. According to a report by one Danish wind engineer, about 20 percent of that country's electrical needs can be met by wind power. This would require hundreds of wind towers, each about 150 feet high.

Even larger wind power projects have been proposed by

Dr. William E. Heronemus, a professor of civil engineering at the University of Massachusetts in Amherst. He suggests that 189 million kilowatts of electricity could be produced by a band of 300,000 wind towers stretching from Texas to North Dakota. Each tower would support 20 turbines and would be 850 feet tall.

Wind power production on this scale would not be a pretty sight, especially when added to the growing "forest" of electric power lines. Also many wind turbines operating in one area might affect the climate. Other environmental problems may be discovered as wind power is studied and developed further. The cost of making and installing modern wind turbines has discouraged development so far. But costs will drop when wind turbines are mass-produced, and wind power will become more competitive as the costs of fossil fuels rise.

LIQUID FUELS

Wind power, along with nuclear, geothermal, and solar power, usually produces energy in the form of electricity. Yet only a small part of the energy used in the United States and other industrial nations is used directly as electricity. Cars and buses run on gasoline, not electricity; large trucks and most trains run on diesel fuel. Fossil fuels, in the form of either liquid or gas, provide most of the nation's energy for transportation, heating, and industry. Even if some of these needs can be met by electricity, there will be a continuing demand for liquid and gaseous fuels.

Part of this need may be met by methanol (see Chapter

3), which can be made from fossil fuels, as well as from garbage, wood, manure, or any other organic material. Part may also be met by hydrogen. Electricity can be used to separate hydrogen from water, through a process called electrolysis. Hydrogen can be used as a fuel directly or mixed with other elements to produce methanol, methane, acetylene, and other hydrocarbon fuels.

Large amounts of energy are needed to produce hydrogen from water. But the need for liquid and gaseous fuels may make large-scale hydrogen production worthwhile. Hydrogen is an ideal fuel in some ways. Liquid hydrogen produces 2.75 times as much energy per pound as jet fuel. Hydrogen is also lighter than petroleum fuels and could replace them in jet planes, where weight is an important factor. Hydrogen has already been tested as a fuel in automobile engines. Dr. Roger J. Schoeppel, an engineer at Oklahoma State University, converted standard car engines to hydrogen fuel. The only wastes produced were steam and nitric oxides (ten times less than the amount produced by an average gasoline engine). Dr. Schoeppel predicted that "the hydrogen-fueled internal-combustion engine vehicle will make its debut before 1977."

A major block to widespread use of hydrogen in cars is fuel storage. Whether liquid or gas, hydrogen takes up much more space than fossil fuels. A car running on hydrogen gas would need a big, heavy storage tank. Several possible solutions to this problem are being studied.

Hydrogen can do nearly all of the jobs done by natural gas. But perhaps its greatest use lies in the role of carrying and storing energy from electricity. Electric power plants usually slow production when demand drops, at night and on weekends, for example. They could operate more efficiently if surplus electricity was changed, by electrolysis of water, to hydrogen fuel and stored for use at peak periods of need for electricity. Hydrogen can also be stored in metal-air batteries, which give more power and recharge more quickly than the lead-acid batteries now used in cars.

Another possible use of hydrogen is in fuel cells. A fuel cell generates electricity through a process that is the reverse of electrolysis—hydrogen and oxygen combine to form water and give off some electric current. The process continues as long as hydrogen and air are supplied to the cell. Fuels other than hydrogen can be used, but this kind of fuel cell is the most efficient and most highly developed so far.

Entire power plants may someday be made of fuel cells. They could be built quickly, and would produce little or no pollution in the air or water. Fuel cells may also be used for energy storage. For example, excess electricity from a nuclear power plant could be used for electrolysis of water, producing hydrogen. Later, when demand for electricity rose, the stored hydrogen could be released into fuel cells, generating electricity as needed.

Hydrogen can be pumped through pipelines, though it has a weakening effect on some metals. Existing natural gas pipelines may not suffice for hydrogen. If sent through pipelines, hydrogen would reduce the need for electric transmission lines and towers, which already resemble metal forests in some areas. Hydrogen may be an especially valuable energy carrier from clusters of nuclear reactors, from solar energy farms, or from various kinds of power plants in the oceans.

ENERGY FROM THE OCEAN

Scientists are looking to the seas more and more as they try to develop new energy supplies. More offshore wells for petroleum and natural gas are expected, of course. Floating nuclear power plants have been proposed. Dr. William E. Heronemus suggests that networks of wind-power stations in the Atlantic Ocean could provide great amounts of energy for the eastern United States. Wind

An artist's view of a floating nuclear power plant, protected from the sea by breakwaters.

The National Science Foundation is investigating ways of converting the heat energy in ocean water to electrical energy. An ocean thermal energy power plant might look like this.

turbines could stand on towers in fairly shallow water or float on platforms farther out to sea. The wind turbines would power the electrolysis process, changing seawater to hydrogen and oxygen. The hydrogen gas could be stored in tanks which could then be shipped to land.

Hydrogen might also be a convenient carrier of energy produced from the temperatures of ocean waters. In the tropics, water near the surface stays near 75°F (25°C) year round. As little as a thousand feet underwater, the temperature is only 41°F (5°C). Like the wind, the varying temperatures of ocean waters are a result of solar energy, so power from this source would be another indirect use of sun energy.

To get electricity from sea water, a huge pipelike structure would be submerged vertically in the water. Hot water would be taken in at the top and used to change liquid propane or ammonia to a gas. After the hot gas was used to turn turbines and generate electricity, it would be cooled back to a liquid by cold ocean water taken in at the base of the "pipe." The turbines would have to be specially designed because of the low pressure and temperature of the gas.

Some small-scale tests of this method have been made during the past 40 years, but many problems still remain. Anchoring the pipelike devices may be difficult, as will protecting them from the corroding seawater. If many of these devices were operating in one area, they might affect water temperatures, with unknown effects on sea life.

It is also possible that the mixing of deep, cold waters

with warmer surface waters will have good effects. Deep ocean waters are rich with nutrients that fish and other living things need for growth and development. The richest harvests of fish are made where deep waters surge to the surface, because these upwellings bring nutrients to the surface where most ocean life exists. One major upwelling, the Humboldt Current off the coast of Peru, supplies one-fifth of the world's total fish catch. An artificial upwelling, produced by pipelike power plants, might increase fish harvests in tropical waters.

Ocean currents themselves might also be a source of electric power. The Florida Current, part of the Gulf Stream, flows northward past Miami and carries more than 50 times the flow of all the rivers in the world. Near the surface the speed of the water is sometimes more than five and one-half miles an hour. A series of underwater turbines might be used to tap some of this power. The large, slow turbines would take only a small part of the total, to avoid disrupting the flow of the Gulf Stream. Energy could also be taken from other currents that flow close to the coasts of continents.

ENERGY FROM TRASH

While reaching far into the oceans and even into space for new sources of energy, scientists are also investigating nearby sources that have been overlooked. Garbage, for instance. It is full of paper, orange rinds, and other organic material which contains energy captured from sunlight.

Pie Crust

Once metals and other valuable materials have been removed for recycling, the remaining wastes can be burned to produce electricity. According to R. Thomas Wilson, of the American Iron and Steel Institute, there's more than a billion dollars worth of energy in trash. He said, "The energy value of the refuse generated every year in the United States is equal to 290 million barrels of low sulfur oil—equal to 5 percent of current domestic oil consumption, or about two-thirds of our foreign imports from Arab countries."

It is unlikely that all of the energy in trash will be recovered, but there is a growing interest in this energy source. The amount of trash itself is growing; cities are running out of places to put it and welcome the idea of burning most of it to produce electricity. Utilities have become more interested in trash because prices of coal and oil have increased so much. As a result, in 1974 a number of utilities and cities in New York, New Jersey, Florida, California, and Ohio were studying ways of generating power from garbage. Connecticut and Massachusetts have adopted plans for statewide systems of recycling plants that will recover metals and produce electricity.

Energy from trash, from geothermal power, and from the sun (for home heating) is likely to play an important role in meeting energy needs by the mid-1980s. But the United States and other industrial nations will still depend on fossil fuels for most of their energy. The fossil fuels will become more scarce and expensive, reminding us that precious time has been lost in the search for substitutes. Engineers, chemists, and other scientists agree that there are no quick energy "fixes." Many years and many billions of dollars are needed to develop energy sources to replace fossil fuels. The era of fossil fuels represents only a brief time in the history of humankind, and we must get on with the search for other energy sources.

The petroleum age is expected to last only two centuries, with supplies dwindling rapidly after world oil production reaches a peak about the year 2000.

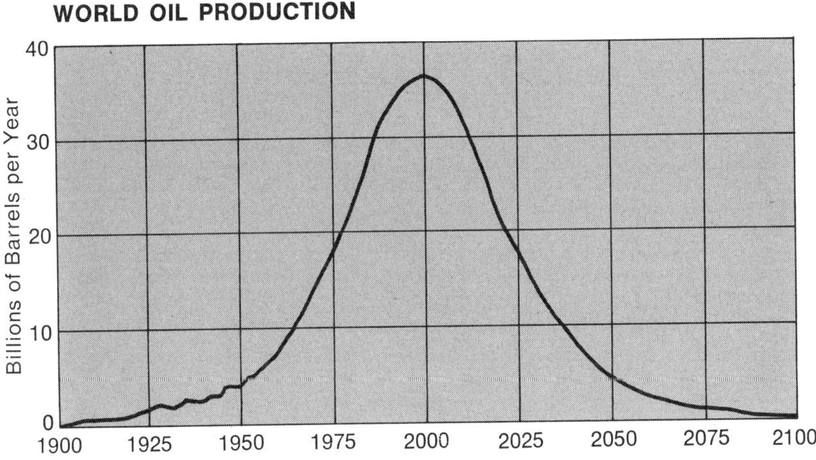

Drawing by MacNelly; © 1973 The Chicago Tribune.

"I Don't Believe It! That Mickey Mouse Power Company Of Ours Is Having Another Power Crisis!"

WASTE NOT, WANT NOT

"Meeting the demands of consumers" is the main reason offered by utilities when they seek permission to build power plants. The same phrase is used by mining, manufacturing, and petroleum companies. Of course, all of these companies stimulate that demand by advertising; this is especially true of the electric power industry. Only after decades of urging people to use more and more power did utilities begin suggesting ways to save energy.

"By 1985 Americans will be consuming twice as much energy as they do today," declared a 1973 oil company advertisement, as though this was a fact, and not a projection. A fast-growing demand for energy was also forecast by the Federal Power Commission (FPC), which estimated that electrical needs would double by 1980 and nearly double again by 1990. And utilities have begun to act upon this projection. Because several years of "lead time" are needed to build a power plant, utilities are planning now for the future. But the Federal Power Commission's prediction, and those of oil and electric industries, are based on the notion that demand for energy will continue to grow as it did during the years 1940–1970. They also assume that energy prices won't rise very much, and that our population will grow rapidly. All of these notions and the projections made from them are open to question.

Population growth in the United States has slowed to the lowest rate since the Census Bureau started keeping figures about 70 years ago. The rate of growth has declined since 1960. And prices of electricity and other forms of energy are rising rapidly. According to a study by the National Science Foundation, if the cost of electricity doubles, the demand for electricity will increase only 33 percent between 1970 and the year 2000—much less than the FPC estimates.

For decades, government and industry leaders have emphasized power production, not power conservation. "We have a National Energy Policy," said S. David Freeman, "and it's basically one of promotion, of pushing the product."

Even in 1973 and 1974, in the midst of serious fuel shortages, many politicians and industry officials continued to speak of meeting demand, not reducing it. But the shortages revealed that demand could be reduced. People heated their homes less and used air conditioning less in the summertime—and the consumption of electricity, natural gas, and fuel oil dropped. Lighting was reduced in schools, businesses, and homes; people found that they could get along fine without the extra light, and great amounts of energy were saved. People began to realize the enormous energy waste that is built into the American lifestyle.

European "longwall" mining machines, which recover nearly all the coal in a mine, are being adopted in the United States.

The waste begins as fuels are taken from the ground. On the average, only about 31 percent of the petroleum in American oil fields is recovered. As petroleum gets scarcer and more expensive, oil companies may find ways to recover more of it. Strip mines and natural gas wells are more efficient, but still fail to recover 20 percent of the fuel. And in some areas, natural gas is still burned as waste. The method of underground coal mining used in the United States is also wasteful, leaving about half of the coal. A method used in Europe recovers up to 90 percent of the coal and is safer for miners. The United States may eventually recover more power from old coal mines and oil fields through the method of *in situ* gasification.

Energy is also wasted when fuel is used. According to the second law of thermodynamics, when energy is transferred or changed, part of it is lost as heat. This happens in machines and also in all living things, including you. Your body gives off 450 Btus an hour while you are resting, and more when you are active. A 4,000-pound car going 70 miles per hour gives off 750,000 Btus in an hour. In each case, chemical energy is being used and some of it is given off as waste heat.

The newest coal-fired power plants are 38 percent efficient; that is, they lose "only" 62 percent of the coal's energy as heat. The average efficiency for all fossil-fueled plants is about 33 percent. Nuclear plants are usually even less efficient.

There are ways of increasing the efficiency of power plants, and it is vital to do so because 25 percent of all fuels consumed in the United States are used to generate electricity. One method is called the combined cycle system. When natural gas is burned to power a turbine, only 25 percent of its energy becomes electricity. But the exhaust gases are quite hot, and can be used to heat water in a boiler, making steam which can then turn another turbine. By combining the gas and steam turbines, the efficiency is raised to 39 percent. Engineers expect that efficiency can go to 50 percent by increasing the operating temperature and adding a third cycle. A study of a combined cycle system for coal estimates that the efficiency would be 51 percent.

The efficiency of power production can also be increased

through a process called magnetohydrodynamics, or MHD. The process has been described as "firing a rocket engine into a magnet." Hot gases from coal or another fuel flow into a generator. The gases are "seeded" with small metal particles which help the gases become electrically charged. When the gases flow through a magnetic field within the generator, the electric charges become a current. In this way, an MHD generator converts hot gases directly into electricity. No energy is lost by heating water to make steam or by turning a turbine. The efficiency of MHD is expected to be near 50 percent. Some engineers estimate it could reach 60 percent if MHD is combined with another cycle, with its hot gases used to produce steam for a turbine after they leave the MHD generator.

Although MHD was first demonstrated in a United States laboratory, research here lagged for lack of money.

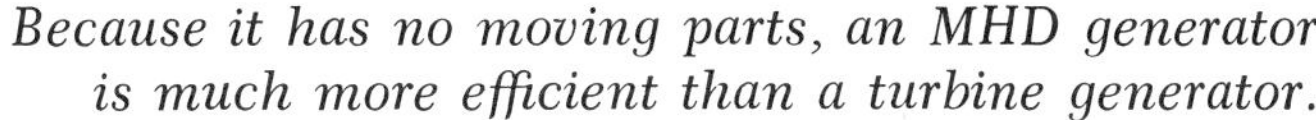

Because it has no moving parts, an MHD generator is much more efficient than a turbine generator.

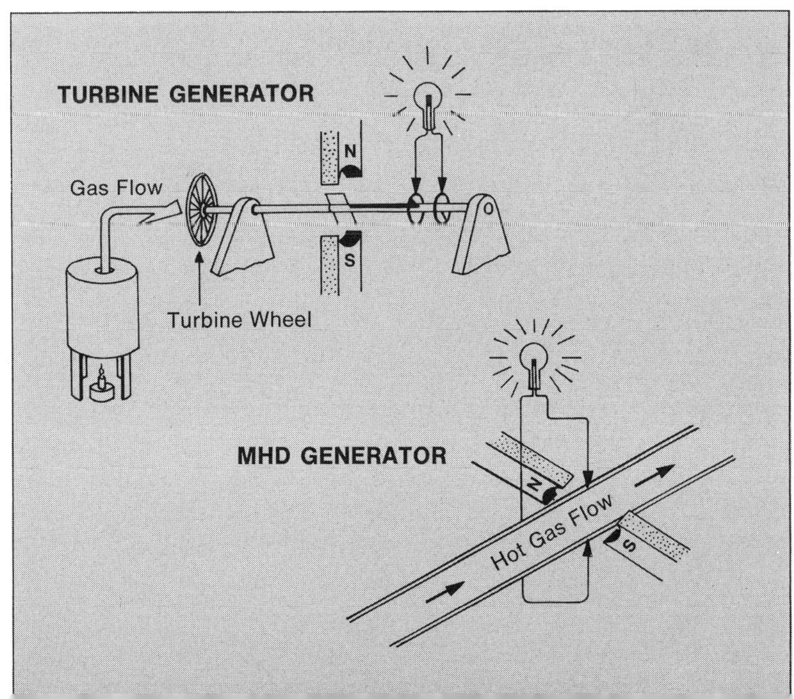

The Soviet Union is already testing an experimental MHD generator fueled by natural gas, and plans to build a giant MHD plant. There are some tough problems yet to be solved. MHD generators must be made of materials that can withstand strong chemicals from their fuels, especially from coal, and temperatures of over 3632°F (2000° C). Years of study and testing in pilot plants are needed before MHD is ready for commercial use. MHD promises to yield up to 20 percent more energy from each ton of coal than produced by conventional power plants; this also means 20 percent less thermal pollution. No wonder scientists urge that more money be spent on MHD development.

The efficiency of electric transmission can also be improved. Energy is lost as heat when electricity flows through power lines. That is one reason that most power lines are aboveground, supported by towers, so that the heat can escape into the air. Power lines put underground must be installed or designed in a way that allows heat to escape, or to reduce heat loss. There is a growing need for underground transmission. In the United States, seven million acres of land are already studded with electric transmission towers, and people object to the towers and lines near their homes and in scenic areas. Since electrical production will increase, underground cables that can carry high voltages are needed. Several kinds are being studied; all of them cost three to five times as much as overhead power lines—another sign that energy prices will rise.

Electric heating of homes and businesses is very inefficient. About 3.3 Btus of energy are taken from fuels at a

power plant in order to produce one Btu in a home. When gas or oil fuels are used directly in homes, only 1.7 Btus are needed to produce one Btu of heat. It is always more efficient to burn fossil fuels directly to product heat, because so much energy is lost as it is changed into electricity and transmitted. However, since supplies of fossil fuels are limited and some are valuable as petrochemicals, many scientists hope that their use for heating can soon be replaced by other forms of energy.

Because of the second law of thermodynamics, it is impossible to use energy and not waste some of it. But there are many opportunities for reducing waste. Consider transportation, for instance. Transportation of people and goods takes about 25 percent of the total United States energy budget. Energy needs for transportation increased by 89 percent between 1950 and 1970. This increase was caused by growing population and traffic but also by people turning to less efficient means of travel—cars and airplanes instead of buses and trains, heavy cars instead of lighter ones.

Three-fourths of the energy from gasoline burned in most American cars is wasted. The standard American car gets about 12 miles per gallon; most European cars get twice as much. The average miles per gallon has declined since World War II, partly because of antipollution devices but mostly because of increased weight and extras like air conditioning and automatic transmission.

Rising gasoline prices and shortages have affected transportation patterns in some areas, as people turned to car pools and mass transit. But great change in transportation will not come easily. The federal government has supported the most wasteful ways of traveling—car and airplane—through funds for highway and airport construction. Auto makers, highway builders, and other powerful industries oppose aid to railroads and mass transit systems. Developing less wasteful ways for travel is vital, though, because 96 percent of the fuel used is petroleum.

Industry is the largest user of energy in the United States, consuming 39 percent. The potential energy savings are huge, and some fast results are possible. In 1974 several companies cut their total energy use by 15 percent or more—by using wastes as fuel, by reducing lighting, by reducing heat in buildings, especially in warehouses and other storage areas, and by turning off machinery and blowers when not in use. Further energy savings in industry are possible but will take longer because they involve changes in machinery or manufacturing processes. One company official said, "It was easy to cut total energy use by 20 percent, and this suggests what enormous waste is built into the American way of doing things. It now seems ridiculous that these steps were not taken long ago."

A 1972 government study called "The Potential for Energy Conservation" reported that energy waste could be cut by 25 to 30 percent over the next 25 years. Some of the savings are quick and easy, others require time, research, and basic change in the way things are done.

Energy conservation can be either "belt tightening" or "leak plugging." "Belt tightening" gets quick results, and

Some industries recover "waste" heat from machines and use it to warm offices.

everyone did some of it when energy shortages began—by using less lighting and heating, thereby reducing energy use in homes and businesses.

"Leak plugging" increases efficiency, by using fluorescent bulbs instead of incandescent bulbs, for example. (Fluorescent bulbs convert 20 percent of the energy they consume into light; incandescent bulbs convert only 5 percent.) One "leak-plugging" step that has a big effect is insulation. Heating, cooling, and lighting of buildings takes about 20 percent of all energy used in the United States. Better insulation in houses can cut heating and cooling needs by 40 to 50 percent. The cost of the insulation can be paid off in four to seven years of reduced fuel bills. The Federal Housing Authority has revised its guidelines for home insulation, and most new homes will be better insulated than older ones. Congress may also consider the idea of offering people special tax benefits if they insulate their older homes.

Big office buildings represent some of the most astonishing examples of energy waste. Sometimes it seems that they have been deliberately designed to waste a maximum amount of energy. In a sense that is true: buildings are usually designed to be built as cheaply as possible, with little attention paid to the cost of operation. The emphasis is on "first cost," not "lifc cost."

Like all energy users, architecture has been on an energy romp for the past few decades. Giant high-rise buildings usually have their broad sides facing east and west, exposing the maximum surface area to the sun. Energy for cooling could be reduced by 30 percent if the broad sides faced north and south. Many modern office buildings have mostly glass walls. Since heat passes easily through glass, these buildings need great amounts of energy for heating in winter and cooling in summer. Heat loss can be cut in half if double panes of glass, with an air space between, are used. Tinted glass also reduces heat loss.

Nearly 20 percent of the energy used in most modern office buildings could be saved by opening the windows and letting air in without heating or cooling it. But windows can't be opened in many buildings. This is true of the twin 110-story towers of the World Trade Center in New York City, which represents a peak of wasteful architecture. None of its 87,200 windows can be opened. It uses more electricity than a city of 100,000 people. Workers cannot control the lights in their offices or even on their own floor because all lighting is operated by a central computer. Rooms with windows usually do not need lights on sunny days, but there is no way to turn off the lights in these rooms without also turning off many other lights.

For many years architects followed the recommendations of the Illumination Engineering Society when planning the lights for a building. The standards of the Illumination Engineering Society have had great effects on the lighting of schools and other buildings. Since 1957 the recom-

Mirror like coatings on glass reflect solar energy and reduce the need for air conditioning in summer.

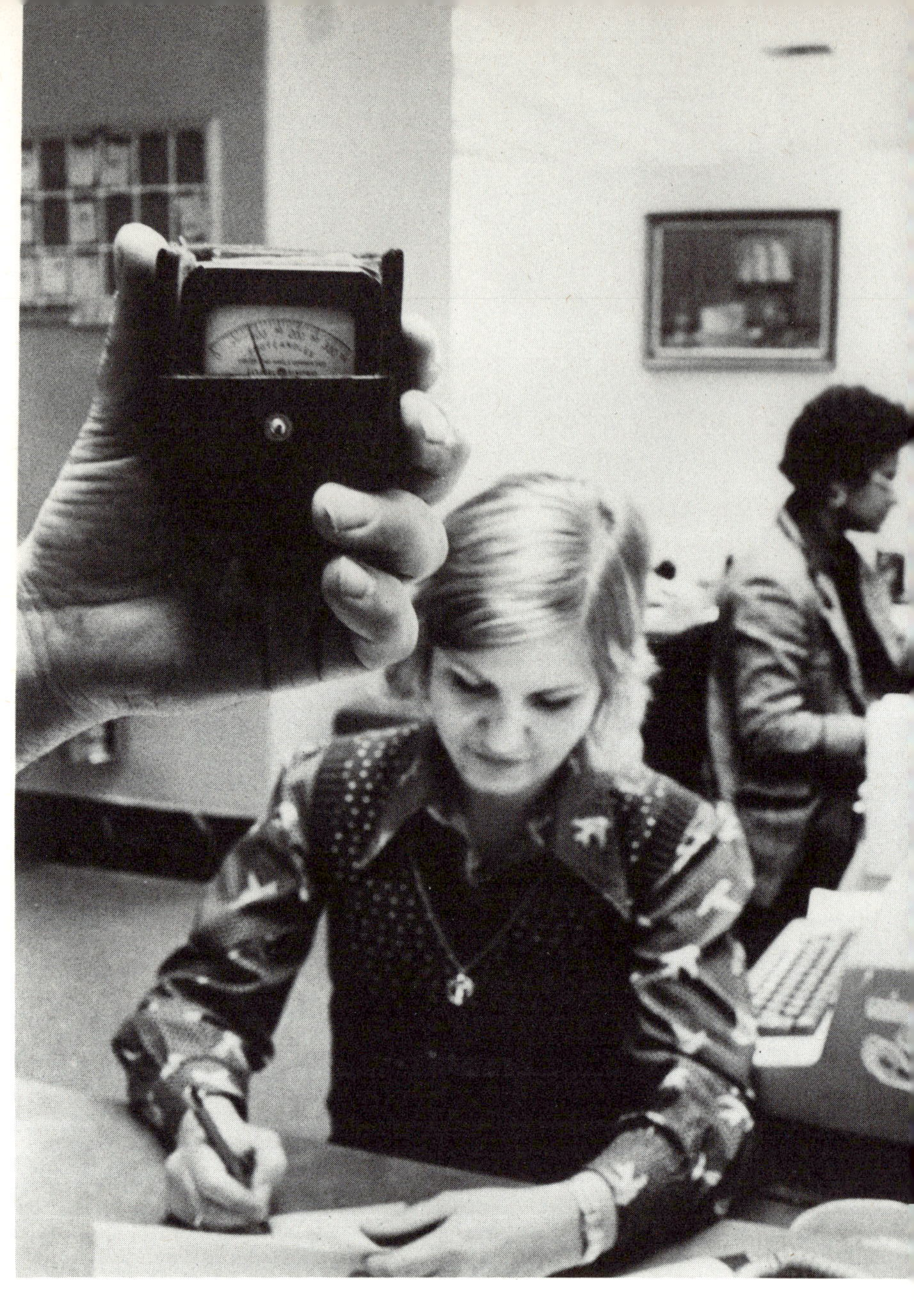

A light meter being used to measure the illumination in an office. In many buildings, lighting is sufficient even when half the bulbs are turned off.

mended lighting level in classrooms has more than doubled. Lighting in commercial buildings has increased even more.

Many architects claim that this lighting is excessive. Some new buildings are so overlit that air conditioning is needed in wintertime to remove waste heat from light bulbs. The standards of the Illumination Engineering Society are being questioned. So are its motives. It seems to have been more interested in promoting the use of electricity and the sale of lighting fixtures and bulbs than in the best lighting for people. According to many architects and lighting engineers, overall lighting levels should be cut in half.

Beginning in 1973, many schools, homes, and commercial buildings saved energy by reducing lighting. And people became more energy conscious about air conditioners and other appliances. There are about 1,400 models of air conditioners sold under 52 different brand names in the United States. The efficiency of these air conditioners varies widely. Some machines use two and a half times as much energy as others that do the same amount of cooling. Many brands now have a number called the energy efficiency ratio (EER). The higher the EER, the greater a machine's efficiency. Usually machines with high EER cost more, but the savings on electric bills makes up the difference in three or four years. According to a study made for the National Science Foundation, power from 7.6 million tons of coal would be saved if all air conditioners had the highest EER.

Toasters, refrigerators, clothes dryers, and other appliances also vary in their efficiency. But people have no way of finding out which model is most efficient. In 1973, a law was introduced in Congress which called for "truth in energy." It would require industries to clearly label the energy efficiency of their products.

Environmentalists believe that there should be a change in utility rates. Rate systems now encourage waste. They favor the customers who use the most energy—businesses and industries—who pay one-third to one-thirtieth as much per kilowatt-hour as others. The big consumers pay less than the true cost of energy, while homeowners and others who use relatively little electricity pay more than the true cost. If everyone paid the same rate, the electric bills of heavy users would rise, and this would encourage them to use energy more efficiently. Another way to charge the true cost of electricity is to use meters that show when power is used. Higher rates could be charged for electricity used during times of peak demand, when it costs more to produce power.

Decisions about many other energy matters must be faced by the federal government. The energy waste that is built into the American lifestyle can be cut drastically, extending the petroleum age for many years. Accomplishing this, however, will bring changes in the ways businesses operate and in the life of every citizen.

Establishing laws to make these changes happen will not be easy; in some cases it may be impossible. Many powerful industries and unions are opposed to change, and their

These four words are a symbol of the throwaway lifestyle, a tremendous waste of energy and resources.

influence on government is often greater than that of the general public. Just because a change will conserve energy and resources does not mean it will be easy to put into effect.

Throwaway containers, for example, are a great waste of valuable metals and glass—and energy. The energy waste per year is equal to 1.7 billion gallons of gasoline. That much energy would be saved if people used returnable bottles for soft drinks and beer. A change back to returnable bottles is opposed by glass and can manufacturers and other industries. And unions oppose the change because some jobs would be lost. But studies have shown that an cqual number of new jobs would be created in other firms as people changed back to the use of returnable bottles.

Most ideas for saving energy will cause some companies to lose business and some workers to lose their jobs, while improving business for other companies and increasing employment in them. Energy shortages have already been a boon to makers of small autos, home insulation, blankets, and efficient air conditioners. Federal and state governments may be able to help ease the path to change by retraining workers for new kinds of jobs.

Other proposals of energy conservation include a special tax on gasoline that would be spent on mass transit systems. One of the most controversial ideas is to set up a Federal Oil and Gas Corporation which would have first choice of fossil fuel leases on federal lands. The corporation would aim to produce energy at the lowest cost possible and would serve as a yardstick for judging the prices and practices of the private oil industry. Many critics of the oil industry suggest that it should be controlled much more by the federal government, especially since oil companies are increasing their hold on all kinds of fuels.

Until 1974 the United States government had no information of its own on the reserves of natural gas and petroleum. The Bureau of Mines and other government agencies had always accepted figures supplied by the petroleum industry. The energy shortages raised doubts about the accuracy of the information and about the good intentions of the oil companies. Many people suspected that energy shortages were deliberately planned, or made worse, by the oil and natural gas producers. The shortages caused rising profits, an easing of air pollution laws, and the elimination of some competition—all to the advantage of the 18 major oil companies that supply most of the nation's

No nation, no matter how rich, can long afford a policy of making products, using them once, then throwing them away.

petroleum and natural gas. As a result, in 1974 the federal government took steps to get its own information on energy supplies. Also, the Federal Trade Commission filed an antitrust suit against the top eight oil companies, accusing them of trying to monopolize the petroleum industry.

Early in 1974, even while people waited in long lines at gasoline stations, some economists warned of "the coming energy glut." They predicted that higher fuel prices would stimulate production, and there would soon be "gasoline coming out of our ears." Shortages were temporary, of course, because there was many years' supply of petroleum in the ground. But energy will probably never be as cheap as it once was, and the end of the petroleum age is not far off. It would be foolish to relax and assume that life can go on as before. S. David Freeman said, "It is naive to believe that Americans can continue indefinitely driving big cars to work and overheating glass buildings with fuel from other nations."

Still, it is difficult to predict or even guess at all of the changes that may take place. What about the suburbs that sprawl out beyond cities? They were built in an era of cheap, plentiful gasoline when many people could easily afford to commute to city jobs by car. Those days may never return. High gasoline prices or a scarcity of gasoline or both could halt suburban sprawl and send many people back to the cities.

Suburbs spread outward from cities when gasoline was cheap and abundant.

Some unpleasant surprises may be ahead. Energy production, especially from new sources, may take a terrible toll of the quality of our environment. Unless the efficiency of energy production and use is improved a lot, waste heat could affect the climate over wide areas.

Americans will discover how much food production depends on energy. Agriculture in the United States is tremendously inefficient, using energy equal to 80 gallons of gasoline in order to produce corn from an acre of land. American agriculture depends heavily on fossil fuels. As the cost of these fuels rises, so will the cost of food.

The United States is fortunate in having some petroleum reserves and rich deposits of coal and oil shale. We have some time left in which to correct past mistakes, begin long-range energy planning, and devote much more money to studies of a wide range of energy sources. There need not be energy shortages, poisons in the air, or an ugly landscape. There is still time to develop clean energy sources, especially if we drop the notion that happiness and prosperity are measured by speed, bigness, and mechanical convenience. In the words of Stewart Udall, it is time to "think small, think slow, think snug."

Great amounts of fossil fuels are used to till the land, make fertilizer, and harvest crops.

Two-wheeled trips save energy and money.

WHAT YOU CAN DO

The possibilities for using less energy in our everyday lives are almost endless. Some ideas are described in the pages of this book; another book would be needed to list them all. Many utilities have free booklets telling of ways to reduce the use of electricity, and some oil companies publish tips on how to use gasoline and heating oil more wisely. Further energy-saving ideas are the subject of several publications listed on pages 139–141.

Once you become "Btu-conscious," you will probably find many ways, big and small, for reducing the use of energy in your life. Here are a few more ideas:

• Half of all gasoline burned by autos is used on trips of three miles or less. By combining such errands, and especially by using bicycles or walking, many gallons of gasoline (and dollars) can be saved.

• If the land surrounding a building is covered by concrete, flagstones, or similar materials that absorb heat from the sun, the temperature at ground level may be 40 to 50 degrees hotter than if the ground was covered with grass or bushes. Nearby plants have a cooling effect on buildings in the summer, and reduce the need for fans and air conditioners.

• Although a border of plants around a house helps save energy, a large, well-kept lawn is usually a tremendous waste of energy. Consider fertilizer, for example. As many as five 50-pound bags may be spread on a 10,000-square-foot lawn each year. It takes 810,000 Btus of natural gas to produce the nitrogen in that fertilizer. Then a half-million Btus of gasoline may be used to mow the lawn, and the nitrogen-rich grass clippings are usually thrown away. Increasing numbers of people are changing at least part of their lawns to vegetable gardens. Grass clippings from the remaining lawn area can be mixed with garbage and soil to make a rich compost, which often eliminates the need for man-made fertilizers.

• On a much smaller scale, be aware of the amount of water that is heated for coffee, tea, or other hot beverages. People often boil a quart of water when they need only a cup or two.

If only a few million people try to stop wasting energy in their day-to-day lives, the effect will be small. If everyone does it, the energy savings will be enormous. Support efforts to spread information about ways of saving energy. Conservation of energy always made sense to some people because it lessened damage to the environment; now it

An energy-conservation advertisement from the Consolidated Edison Company of New York City.

THE ENERGY CRISIS STRIKES HOME

So here are 10 effective ways you can strike back:

1

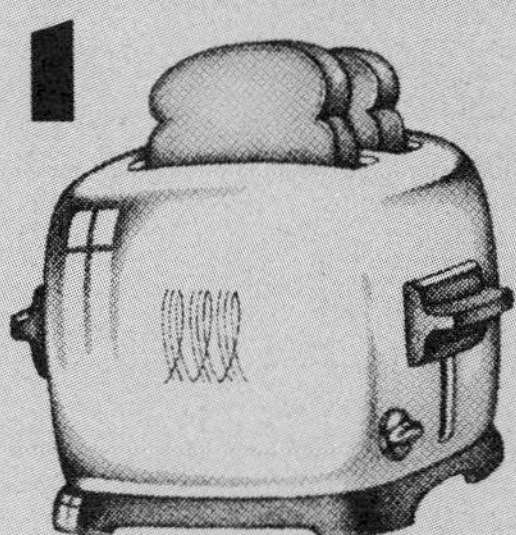

Run most appliances before 8 a.m. or after 6 p.m.

2

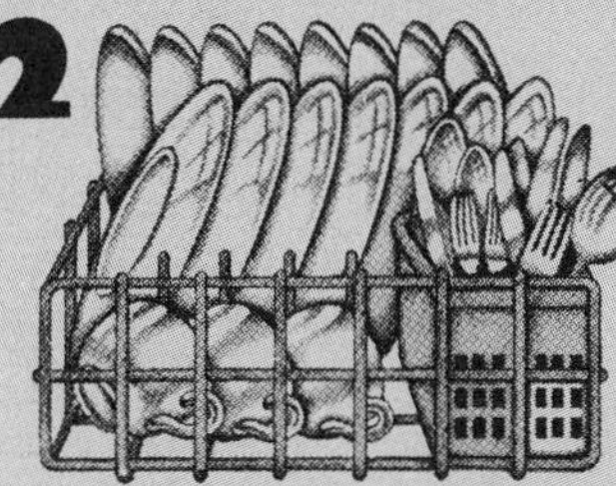

Use your dishwasher only after the evening meal.

3

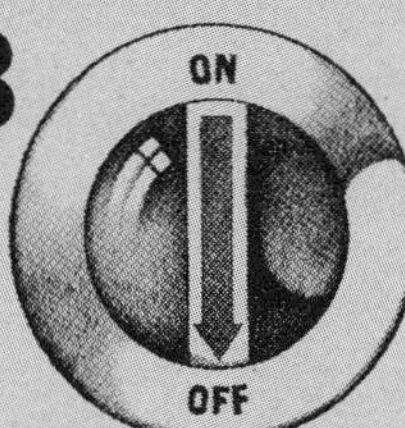

Turn off the air conditioner when no one is home.

4

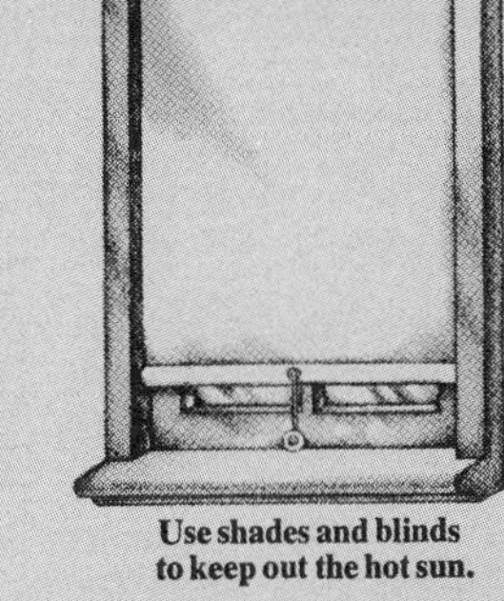

Use shades and blinds to keep out the hot sun.

5

Buy an air conditioner that's the right size and highly efficient.

6

Turn off the TV and radio when you're not looking or listening.

7

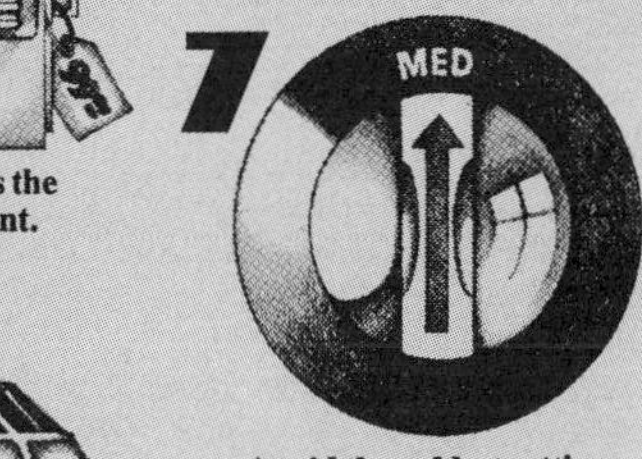

Avoid the coldest settings on the air conditioner.

8

Turn off the kitchen range or oven when not in use.

9

Keep lights off when not needed for safety, health or comfort.

10

Use the washer and dryer only on weekends or evenings.

The national energy crisis has struck home. Your home. You see, it takes a lot of fuel (mostly oil and gas in Con Edison's case) to produce the electricity required by Con Edison customers. And the fuel shortage is at the heart of the energy crisis.

So Con Edison continues to ask its customers to use electricity wisely. Keep the energy crisis in mind when you turn on an electric appliance... from light bulbs to air conditioners.

To make the point even plainer, here are two extreme examples: Suppose you leave just one room-size air conditioner on night and day all summer long. You could waste as much as 300 gallons of oil, not to mention up to $135.00 extra on your electric bill.

Again, suppose you left on ten 100-watt light bulbs around the clock for one year. You could waste over 600 gallons of oil . . . not to mention $280.00 extra on your electric bill.

This is the third year Con Edison has been asking its customers to Save-A-Watt and suggesting 10 important ways to go about it. But this year the national energy crisis adds a new note of urgency.

Con Edison conserve energy

save-a-watt

makes economic sense to almost everyone. People will become increasingly interested in energy conservation as the costs of fuels and electricity rise.

But the efforts of individuals and families can only accomplish so much. The unofficial policy of government and industry has been to emphasize energy production, not conservation. At all levels of government there are countless laws and other regulations that encourage the waste of energy. It is in the public interest to change these rules, but the change will not come easily. All too often, government leaders ignore the public interest and favor industries and other powerful groups that are opposed to change.

You can help bring about real change by arousing the interest of other people. Once you are well-informed about ways for saving energy, write letters to newspapers and to legislators. Create an exhibit at the local library. Join environmental groups or other organizations that are trying to stop energy waste, either locally or nationally.

In local and state government, there may be building codes that can be changed so that new homes use energy more efficiently. Tax laws can be changed to reward people who insulate older homes or who install solar heating and cooling systems. In the federal government, present laws and policies often discourage the development of mass transit, greater recycling of resources, and research in energy conservation. Only the combined efforts of many people will convince elected officials to change these laws and policies.

WHAT YOU CAN DO

GLOSSARY

BREEDER—a nuclear reactor that produces more fuel than it consumes. Breeders use uranium 235 or plutonium as fuel. Neutrons produced by the fission of these elements react with uranium 238, converting it to plutonium, which can then be used as more fuel.

BRITISH THERMAL UNIT (Btu)—the amount of energy needed to raise the temperature of one pound of water by one degree Fahrenheit at or near 39.2°F (4°C).

COMBINED CYCLE POWER PLANT—a power plant in which two or more different kinds of turbines are used to get the maximum amount of work from the burning of a fuel. Combined cycle systems are more efficient than ordinary power plants, and thus reduce waste heat.

ELECTROLYSIS—the breakdown of a compound into its elements by passing an electric current through an electrolyte (such as a salt solution) containing the compound. Electrolysis of water produces its two elements, hydrogen and oxygen.

ENERGY—the capacity or ability to do work. It may be mechanical, thermal, radiant, chemical, electrical, or nuclear.

ENVIRONMENT—all of the surroundings of an organism, including other living things, soil, and climate.

FISSION—the splitting of the nuclei of a heavy element such as uranium. Fission releases heat energy and is the process used in all nuclear power plants built so far.

FUEL CELL—a battery or electrochemical cell in which a fuel is changed directly to electric energy, with nearly twice the efficiency of ordinary electric generators.

FUSION—a nuclear reaction in which two light atomic nuclei combine (fuse) to form a heavier, more stable nucleus, and release energy. The energy of stars, including our sun, comes from fusion reactions.

GEOTHERMAL—heat within the earth, caused by the decay of radioactive elements far below the surface.

HYDROFRACTURING—the use of water, pumped underground under great pressure, to form underground openings or channels in order to free trapped natural gas or petroleum.

HYDROELECTRIC—power produced by converting the energy of falling water to electricity.

IN SITU ENERGY PRODUCTION—producing oil from shale or gases from coal "in place," without mining the shale or coal. The process has not yet been developed commercially.

MAGNETOHYDRODYNAMIC (MHD) GENERATOR—an engine in which a hot, electricity-conducting gas is forced through a magnetic field to generate an electric current. This is a more efficient way of producing electricity than burning fuel to heat water to steam, which powers the turbine in an electric generator.

METHANOL—an odorless, colorless liquid fuel which can be made from natural gas, petroleum, coal, wood, or farm and city wastes. It is also called methyl alcohol, wood alcohol, or methylated spirits.

MINE MOUTH POWER GENERATION—electricity produced near coal mines or other sources of fuel, then transmitted to cities. This method is sometimes more economical than shipping the fuel long distances.

NUCLEAR POWER—*see* FISSION, FUSION

OIL SHALE—a fine-grained sedimentary rock which contains an oil-yielding organic material called kerogen. The best oil shale in the United States yields less than 30 gallons of oil from a ton of rock.

PETROCHEMICALS—compounds of mostly carbon and hydrogen, made by chemical conversion of natural gas, petroleum, or oil refinery products. Petrochemicals include ammonia, acetylene, ethylene, benzene, toluene, naphthalene, and pentane. They are used in thousands of products.

PHOTOVOLTAIC CELL—a "battery" in which light energy striking certain crystals dislodges electrons from their atoms. The electrons can then be drawn off as an electric current. Photovoltaic cells are used in exposure meters (for photography) and in satellites. The crystals used are silicon, cadmium sulfide, or gallium arsenide.

PILOT PLANT—a small industrial plant used to test or develop a new process. A pilot plant's capacity is usually between 1 and 10 percent of a full-scale commercial plant.

PLUTONIUM—a silvery radioactive element, traces of which

occur in uranium ores. It can also be made artifically from uranium 238. Plutonium is one of the most potent poisons known; a tiny dustlike particle can cause lung cancer.

PYROLYSIS—the process of breaking down chemical compounds by heating them, usually in the absence of air. Also called destructive distillation.

RADIOACTIVITY—the property of giving off energy spontaneously from atoms. This occurs naturally in a few elements and also can be produced artificially.

REFINING—the separation of petroleum, or crude oil, into lighter oils. The compounds, or fractions, within petroleum boil at different temperatures, so they can be separated one by one as the temperature rises. The main fractions are gasoline, naphtha, kerosene, gas oils, and residual fuel oils. More gasoline can be produced by "cracking" the molecules of heavy oils.

SOLAR ENERGY—energy produced by thermonuclear reactions of the sun. The earth intercepts less than one-billionth of the sun's energy, but this energy produced all fossil fuels, causes the winds and ocean currents, and produces all food on earth.

TURBINE—a rotary engine that is turned by the push of a liquid or gas. The simplest examples are a waterwheel and a windmill.

FURTHER READING

Books and magazine articles marked with an asterisk (*) are fairly simple; the others are more difficult.

*ANONYMOUS, "How to Cut Fat Out of Your Home Energy Budget." *Smithsonian*, March 1974, pp. 54–64. Tips on reducing energy use in homes.

BERG, GEORGE G., "Hot Wastes from Nuclear Power." *Environment*, May 1973, pp. 36–44. The problems of handling and storing radioactive wastes from nuclear power plants.

*CENTER FOR ECONOMIC AND SOCIAL INFORMATION, "Oil and the Poor Countries." *Environment*, March 1974, pp. 10–14. Developing nations are hardest hit by rising oil prices.

CLARK, WILSON, *Energy for Survival*. New York: Doubleday & Company, Inc., 1974. A comprehensive study of current energy problems and alternatives to petroleum.

*FARNEY, DENNIS, "Ominous Problem: What to Do with Radioactive Waste." *Smithsonian*, April 1974, pp. 20–27. Details on the kinds of wastes produced and various plans for "disposal."

*FENNER, DAVID, and KLARMANN, JOSEPH, "Power from the

Earth." *Environment*, December 1971, pp. 19–26, 31–34. A detailed report on geothermal energy.

FREEMAN, S. DAVID, *Energy: The New Era.* New York: Walker & Company, 1974. An analysis of the United States' energy problems, with suggestions for a national energy policy.

*GROVE, NOEL, "Oil, the Dwindling Treasure." *National Geographic*, June 1974, pp. 792–825. Where petroleum comes from, how it is used, and the prospects for new sources.

HAMMOND, ALLEN L., *et al.*, *Energy and the Future.* Washington, D.C.: American Association for the Advancement of Science, 1973. A collection of 18 technical articles on future energy sources, energy transmission, and energy conservation.

*KASPER, WILLIAM C., "Power from Trash." *Environment*, March 1974, pp. 34–38. Explains how solid wastes can make a modest but important addition to energy supplies.

LANDSBERG, H. H., "Low-Cost, Abundant Energy: Paradise Lost?" *Science*, April 19, 1974, pp. 247–253. An introduction to a special issue on energy, with articles on energy conservation, coal gasification, geothermal and solar energy, and many other topics.

LARGE, DAVID B., ed., *Hidden Waste: Potentials for Energy Conservation.* Washington, D.C.: The Conservation Foundation, 1973. A study of opportunities for energy conservation in homes, other buildings, transportation, and industry.

*MCCAULL, JULIAN, "Windmills." *Environment*, January–February 1973, pp. 6–17. Plans and prospects for developing wind power.

NOVICK, SHELDON, "Toward a Nuclear Power Precipice." *Environment*, March 1973, pp. 32–40. Describes the unsolved problems of nuclear development, including theft, accidents, and waste disposal.

OFFICE OF EMERGENCY PREPAREDNESS, *The Potential for Energy Conservation*. October 1972. A government study available from the United States Government Printing Office, Washington, D.C. 20402.

*PRINGLE, LAURENCE, *Recycling Resources*. New York: Macmillan Publishing Co., Inc., 1974. Includes information on the use of trash as a source of electricity.

ROBERTS, KEITH, ed., *Towards an Energy Policy*. San Francisco: The Sierra Club, 1973. A collection of 18 papers given at a 1972 energy conference, available from the Sierra Club, 1050 Mills Tower, San Francisco, California 94104.

ROSE, DAVID J., "Energy Policy in the United States." *Scientific American*, January 1974, pp. 20–29. Analyzes the energy "policy" so far and points out the folly of research emphasis on nuclear breeder reactors.

*SOUCIE, GARY, "Oil Shale: Pandora's New Box." *Audubon*, January 1972, pp. 106–112. The oil shale riches in the western United States, and the environmental problems development may bring.

TAMPLIN, ARTHUR R., "Solar Energy." *Environment*, June 1973, pp. 16–20. The prospects and problems of solar energy development.

*WEAVER, KENNETH, "The Search for Tomorrow's Power." *National Geographic*, November 1972, pp. 650–681. A well-illustrated article on the search for future energy supplies.

INDEX

Asterisk (*) indicates photograph or drawing

PICTURE CREDITS

Alyeska Pipeline Service Co., 7, 11, 32-33; American Gas Association, 31; American Telephone & Telegraph Co., 114, 118; Bettmann Archive, 36; Brace Research Institute, 93; Consolidated Edison of New York, 131; Danske Elvaerkers Forening, 92; Exxon Corporation, 3; French Embassy, 70; Gulf Oil Corporation, 18; Honeywell, Inc., 84, 89; Libby-Owens-Ford Co., 117; Arthur D. Little Inc., 87; Mobil Oil Corporation, 14, 29; National Coal Association, 107; National Science Foundation, 98; Offshore Power Systems, 97; Pacific Gas & Electric Co., 73, 74; Princeton University Plasma Physics Laboratory, 67; Laurence Pringle, 13, 101, 111, 121, 124, 128; Research-Cottrell, 57; David Sumner, 26, 91; Tass from Sovfoto, 25; U.S. Atomic Energy Commission, 52, 58, 63, 68; U.S. Department of Agriculture, 127; U.S. Environmental Protection Agency—Documerica, 40 (Leroy Woodson), 123 (Bill Gillette), 133 (Gene Daniels); U.S. Department of the Interior: Bureau of Land Management, 21; —, Bureau of Mines, 39 (top), 43; —, Bureau of Reclamation, 39 (top), 48; University of Delaware, 82; Wide World Photos, viii, 8. Drawings and diagrams by Sylvia Allman: 17, 22, 45 (adapted from Gulf Oil Corp.), 47 (adapted from *Popular Science*), 54, 55 (adapted from U.S. Atomic Energy Commission), 66, 79 (adapted from U.S. Atomic Energy Commission), 85 (adapted from Honeywell, Inc.), 103, 109.

ALSO BY LAURENCE PRINGLE

Ecology:
Science of Survival

Estuaries:
Where Rivers Meet the Sea

From Pond to Prairie

Into the Woods

One Earth, Many People:
The Challenge of Human Population Growth

The Only Earth We Have

Pests and People:
The Search for Sensible Pest Control

Recycling Resources

This Is a River